A Dark Magician Meets a Victorian Sleuth

Leigh Blackmore

RANDALL COLLINS. *The Case of the Philosophers' Ring by Dr John H. Watson: A Novel*. Brighton, UK: Harvester Press, 1980. 152 pp.

Sometimes the boundaries of horror fiction are wider than we readily admit. A vintage novel I had heard of for years before reading it is *The Case of the Philosophers' Ring*. My main interest in reading it was the matchup between the renowned (some would say infamous) magician Aleister Crowley and the Victorian sleuth (probably the most famous sleuth of all) Sherlock Holmes. While this meeting of real and fictional personalities does not make for a "conventional" horror novel, *The Case of the Philosophers' Ring* can perhaps be regarded as a "slipstream" volume in the genre, especially once Crowley comes on the scene. Even though it was published many years ago, it is worth drawing attention to, since the author has provided an agreeable mixture of horror and mystery within its pages.

In this short novel, it is the summer before the outbreak of World War I. Sherlock Holmes, at his Baker Street flat, receives a telegram from the brilliant young philosopher Bertrand Russell, begging him to come to Cambridge to investigate the theft of a uniquely precious treasure—the mind of Ludwig Wittgenstein. According to the dust jacket copy, "thus begins one of the most diabolically clever, suspense-laden imaginings of the Sherlock Holmes legend." Perhaps this is overstating the case, for while the book is enjoyable and intelligently written, it has several failings. The "Philosophers' Ring" of the title is not a piece of jewelry, but a circle of Cambridge scholars including G. H. Hardy, John Maynard Keynes, and G. E. Moore. As Holmes and Watson set out to investigate some of the world's greatest minds, they encounter these personalities up close. However, while the author's knowledge of, and research on, these figures is evident, the characters are too sketchily portrayed. For the first half of the book there is a demonstrable weakness in characterization as the author introduces one after the other of these characters and (together with the Indian mathematician Ramanujan, who dies under suspicious circumstances) parades them on the page in what amounts to a series of brief caricatures.

Holmes and Watson themselves are somewhat sketchily drawn as well. Holmes often draws deeply on his pipe and speculates as to the possible solution to the goings-on, but his ratiocinative faculties are in small evidence. Watson, apart from conveying the narrative, is virtually invisible, and we do not gain that sense of the strong bond of friendship between the two men that is so essential in the Canon.

As the story proceeds, Watson and Holmes cross paths with several figures of the late nineteenth-century esoteric movements, including Annie Besant and C. W. Leadbeater of the Theosophical Society. In the second half of the novel, the Edwardian mystic and magician Aleister Crowley comes to the fore as the probable villain behind the sinister doings. Collins has done his research on Crowley pretty well and manages to put into Crowley's mouth many of the sentiments that were featured in his religio-political system of Thelema, as well as focusing on Crowley's disciple, the young violinist Leila Waddell, "The Scarlet Woman," who quotes from Crowley's key text *The Book of the Law*. Some clues center on the nature of Crowley's magical seal (reproduced several times in the text) and the purposes of his magical order, the Order of the Silver Star (A.A.). There are intrigues around the supply of various drugs, which apparently stem back to Crowley and his associates. If Crowley is depicted mainly as the stereotypical "wickedest man in the world," one can, I suppose, forgive the author, since in most matters he depicts Crowley accurately, if in an unflattering light.

Holmes shows throughout the tale what many would consider a disturbing inclination to be open to various matters of occult lore and psychic phenomena. While throwing the Holmes-Watson team against the notorious magician promis-

DEAD RECKONINGS

A Review of Horror and the Weird in the Arts
Edited by Alex Houstoun and Michael J. Abolafia
No. 36 (Fall 2024)

3   A Return to Horrific Form .... Greg Gbur
    Laird Barron, *Not a Speck of Light*.

5   A Dark Magician Meets a Victorian Sleuth ..... Leigh Blackmore
    Randall Collins, *The Case of the Philosophers' Ring by Dr John H. Watson: A Novel*.

8   Some Notes on a Necroentity: Reflections on
    NecronomiCon Providence 2024 .... Edward Guimont

10 Ramsey's Rant: Taking My Shape .... Ramsey Campbell

15 The Hollowing of Hatred .... Géza A. G. Reilly
    Scott R. Jones, *Drill*.

18 Traducteur pour Le Fantastique: Brian Stableford, 1948–
    2024 .... The joey Zone

23 Ligotti and the Tradition of Wishful Selfhood ....
                                                            Katherine Kerestman

30 Midsummer Shamblings: NecronomiCon Providence et al.....
                                                            Darrell Schweitzer

38 The Four-Fifteen Express .... Amelia B. Edwards

65 Ars Necronomica 2024: A Portal into Bleakness and
    Wonder .... The joey Zone

69 The Canadian Brick Wall .... Géza A. G. Reilly
    Michael Kelly, ed., *Northern Nights*.

72 A Truly Haunting Haunting .... Darrell Schweitzer
    David Lowry, dir., *A Ghost Story*.

74 Cultists Invade Providence: Reflections on NecronomiCon
    2024 .... David T. Zeppieri

78 The Lingering Shadow of World War II .... S. T. Joshi
    Ramsey Campbell, *The Incubations*.

82 Portable Gothic: A Few Thoughts on Place..........................
    Karen Joan Kohoutek

85 Updating Blackwood's "The Willows" ..... Darrell Schweitzer
    T. Kingfisher, *The Hollow Places.*

89 "The Earth Alone Lasts:" The Myth of Meaning in the
    Speculative Fiction of Robert W. Chambers..........................
    Katherine Kerestman
    Robert W. Chambers, *Robert W. Chambers,* ed. S. T. Joshi.

96 When Everything Is Wrong and Nothing Is for Anyone.......
    Géza A. G. Reilly
    Robert Guffey, *The Expectant Mother Disinformation Handbook.*

100 About the Contributors

DEAD RECKONINGS is published by Hippocampus Press, P.O. Box 641, New York, NY 10156 (www.hippocampuspress. com). Copyright © 2024 by Hippocampus Press. Cover art by Jason C. Eckhardt. Cover design by Barbara Briggs Silbert. Hippocampus Press logo by Anastasia Damianakos. Orders and subscriptions should be sent to Hippocampus Press. Contact Alex Houstoun at deadreckoningsjournal@gmail.com for assignments or before submitting a publication for review.

ISSN 1935-6110   ISBN 9781614984634

A Return to Horrific Form

Greg Gbur

LAIRD BARRON. *Not a Speck of Light.* Brookings, SD: Bad Hand Books, 2024. 372 pp. $19.99 tpb. ISBN: 9798218036065.

It has been quite some time since we had a novel or collection of pure horror from Laird Barron. His last collection in the genre was the excellent *Swift to Chase* (2016), which also introduced us to his "final girl" protagonist Jessica Mace; his last longer work in horror was the pulp adventure/horror mashup *X's for Eyes*, which was published in 2015. Since then, he has focused on his Isaiah Coleridge series of crime novels, starting with *Blood Standard*, released in 2018.

Finally, after nearly a decade hiatus, Barron has returned to the horror genre with the collection *Not a Speck of Light*, published by Bad Hand Books. Fans of Barron's work will be happy to know that he still has a talent for the strange and horrific, though his style has evolved with the passage of time.

Those who have been following Barron's career know that he fell critically ill in 2022 and is still recovering from that nearly fatal illness. At a glance, it was tempting for me to assume that his return to horror was spurred on by that experience, but that is not quite true: he in fact never left the horror genre. The stories in this collection range from 2015 to 2021, and it appears that he only stopped writing horror when he was physically unable. As Barron himself recounts in the afterword to the collection, his illness may have motivated him to get this next collection into print.

Not a Speck of Light consists of sixteen tales, though the last one serves more as a short coda to the collection than a full tale. As in his previous collection, *Swift to Chase,* the stories are divided into sections roughly based on their subject: "Blood Red Samaritans," "Wandering Stars," "Alan Smithee Is Dead," and "Lake Terror." These titles don't give a clear indication of the theme of each section, but stories are often connected to one another, usually in unexpected ways.

The stories are varied in topic, ranging from apocalyptic horror to classic ghost stories to existential horror to cosmic horror. The influence of Barron's crime fiction writing on the collection is apparent in many of the stories, which include hard-boiled protagonists. Several of the stories feature Barron's recurring character Jessica Mace, referred to as a "professional final girl," in that she has a supernatural proclivity to get into horrific and deadly circumstances and come out on the other side alive, albeit not unscathed. Many of the stories feature the haunting remoteness of the Alaskan wilderness, and many of them also feature canine companions in leading or supporting roles.

I found all the stories compelling and satisfying, but here are a few of the highlights for me personally. In "In a Cavern, In a Canyon," an old woman recounts her near-miss encounter with a supernatural horror of her youth . . . and her expectation that the encounter would not be her last. "Girls Without Their Faces On" features what may be the worst romantic date of all time, when a woman realizes that her boyfriend may be involved in bringing about the end of the world. In "Fear Sun," a wealthy and corrupt woman describes how she came about constructing a Lovecraftian Innsmouth-themed resort town for the amusement of literally unfathomable powers. "Don't Make Me Assume My Ultimate Form" leads us on a special agent's mission to recover a mysterious person or object—"you'll know it when you see it"—and failure may result in the fiery end of the planet. In "Tiptoe," a man's childhood trauma is awakened by a seemingly random event that leads him to recall a childhood game he played with his father and the sinister implications of that game.

All the stories have a dreamlike, nightmarish quality, and in some of them it is difficult to ascertain what exactly is happening. This is clearly deliberate and evokes an additional sense of unease for the reader. These stories are Barron at his strangest and most experimental: I would not recommend this as the first collection for a reader new to Barron, but it is worth the experience for anyone familiar with his work. Hopefully we won't have to wait another near-decade to get more of Barron's weird visions collected into print.

Note: The author is an acquaintance of Barron's on social media, though they have never met in person.

es to be a thrilling adventure, Randall Collins does not fully deliver on this promise. True, the detectives track Crowley to his London home, and later to his Abbey of Thelema in Cefalu, Sicily; but what rich material might have been made of this is largely vitiated by the brevity of the treatment.

The Case of the Philosophers' Ring is, to my knowledge, the only novel to feature both Holmes and Crowley, and while it is commendable that Collins (apart from a few anachronistic touches) sticks to the main facts of the magician's life and work, the story could well have been told at greater depth than its slim 152 pages permits. Nevertheless, it is an enjoyable *jeu d'esprit* in the tradition of Holmesian pastiches, and will be enjoyed by anyone who is an enthusiast of the Apostles Club of Cambridge (Bertrand Russell and his confrères), of the mystical-magical scene of pre–World War I London, and by those who enjoy seeing Holmes and Watson triumph in the end. Following page 152, several pages of black and white plates reproduce photographs of some of the main "real life" players, including Russell, Keynes, Crowley, Lytton Strachey and Virginia Woolf, and Leila Waddell. Recommended, with some reservations.

Some Notes on a Necroentity: Reflections on NecronomiCon Providence 2024

Edward Guimont

NecronomiCon is always an event to look forward to, not just for the chance to indulge in the joys of Lovecraftiana and the weird with scores of like-minded pilgrims to the Storied City, but for me, as a professor, it also symbolizes the end of summer and the arrival of the new academic year. 2024 was my fifth NecronomiCon, more than many—though, as I realized, there are also still quite a few veterans of the earlier 1990s incarnation in attendance. Still, five NecronomiCons means that there is now a third reason to enjoy its arrival: the chance to see recognizable faces and catch up with now-familiar comrades. I am luckier than most in that I live only a short car ride from Providence, and so visit Lovecraft Arts and Sciences and its crew often, but in the opening day I was able to see both Fred Lubnow and Elena Tchougounova-Paulson, two steadfast Lovecraftian academics, again for the first time since 2022. In expanding the circle of attendees, this was also the first year I was attending with a friend, David Zeppieri, who came from Connecticut and stayed with me during the course of the convention. We spent Thursday morning on a perambulation of Providence, including a few of the Lovecraftian sites on College Hill, where I noticed that a very energetic Goldendoodle now lives at Lovecraft's 65 Prospect Street house. I wonder what the cat lover would make of that (or of the breed that didn't exist in his lifetime).

This was Elena's first year in her new role as Armitage Symposium chair, and my first time since 2015 that I was not taking part in the Armitage. But that was because this was the first year I also took on a new role: the head of the academic speakers' track. While we had some last-minute cancellations and unavailabilities, the presentations we did get were very well attended and received. Andrew Davinack and Carolyn

Tepolt gave a joint and graphic presentation on their research into oceanic parasites, and I presented on my upcoming book, *The Power of the Flat Earth Idea*. On the topic of books, this is also the first NecronomiCon since my debut book, *When the Stars Are Right: H. P. Lovecraft and Astronomy* (co-written with Horace Smith, who unfortunately could not attend), was released by Hippocampus. Getting to sign copies of my book at the Hippocampus booth in the vendor hall was a new experience, as was having people show me the copies they bought. It made me reflect that the Old Gent never had the chance to experience that validation.

Outside of the formal academic talks, I also sat on several panels—Hollow Earth (which I moderated), Zothique, atomic age horror—which not only produced fun discussions among panelists and audiences, but also gave me the chance to chat with some big names—Darrell Schweitzer, Will Murray, Dan Harms. In the vendors' hall, I also had a pleasant chat with Jim Dyer, the grandson of C. M. and Muriel Eddy, who mentioned that C. M. was cousin of 1930s actor Nelson Eddy and more distantly related to musician Duane Eddy, two connections I had never seen before.

I was not alone in thinking that this NecronomiCon was more packed than previous years, in both people and events, even outside the new 8 A.M. opening bloc. I could easily take up a considerable chunk of this issue describing every intriguing event and wonderful conversation I had over those four days. I will sadly have to skip over the opening ceremony, the fantastic (as always) HPLHS Dark Adventure Radio Theater performances, and the engaging Trinity Brewhouse trivia night. But I will appropriately end on what was the end of the convention. In previous years, due to scheduling, I had never been able to take part in the interactive, live-music showing of the 1970 film adaptation of *The Dunwich Horror*. This year I was finally able to do so, the first time it was done in an outside setting. Enjoying a Narragansett beer and popcorn while chatting with new friends, promising to stay in touch as Dean Stockwell chanted "Yog-Sothoth!" and the aliens of Big Nazo danced about, was probably the best introduction to that movie, and the best way to end NecronomiCon 2024 with lots of excitement for 2026.

Ramsey's Rant: Taking My Shape

Ramsey Campbell

I'm no longer wholly sure which was the first anthology I read, although I graduated to reading adult books when I was six. My mother set me loose with her tickets in the local public library—Childwall, housed back then in the midst of a terrace of shops by the Fiveways roundabout, and consisting of a long narrow room with shelves mounted on three walls and an elongated two-faced bookcase dividing the premises. I assume she felt any books such places stocked had been vetted for acceptability, and in general the librarians let me borrow what I liked (even *Lord of the Flies* when Schuyler Miller's review in *Astounding* alerted me to its existence). Indeed, I remember them drawing just one line, at Gogol's *Dead Souls*, a title that had suggested the spectral to me. They and my mother can hardly have read some of the books I took home, and I believe much of my reading shaped how I would go on to write.

It started with the first such book, either *50 Years of Ghost Stories* or *Great Short Stories of the World*. Both contained tales that haunted me for years. If the latter book was the first I read of the pair, then Pliny's story of the haunted house must have been my initial encounter with ghostly fiction. While familiarity may have rusted the clamorous chains, the motif of the suspiciously underpriced house is with us still; I confess to using it in my most recently completed novel. It's only now I realise, having revisited the anthology, where I first found the time-honoured trope.

I believe the six-year-old Campbell homed in mostly on the tales that promised the macabre. I read of the dead but loquacious Mrs Veal and of the terribly strange bed, but it was "The Tell-Tale Heart" that pushed horror and its youthful reader close to the edge. Yet the story that lodged deepest in my mind was Stephen Crane's "A Dark-Brown Dog," and its unflinching naturalism—the child's behaviour towards the animal, the treatment the dog receives in the cramped tenement accommodation, the vivid circumstantial detail of the bleak finale—stayed with me. Well into my adulthood I was convinced it was one of Arthur Morrison's tales of mean streets, but the book represents those with a different selection. I'm inclined to think the Crane, like Buñuel's *Los Olvidados*, may have helped form my commitment to social realism.

By contrast, *Fifty Years of Ghost Stories* fixed my fascination with the spectral. Edith Wharton's prose presented no problems, and the reason for her title "Afterward" left me with an authentic chill. An excised chapter introduced me to Dracula years before I found a copy of the novel, and—along with "The Haunted and the Haunters"—to relishing the extravagantly uncanny. The images that loomed over my bed in the dark for nights if not weeks, however, were more insidiously suggestive: the little hand that gropes out of a stack of linen in a drawer, the insectoid feelers that fumble at their victim's face in an unlit room. My reaction was that of the horror aficionado: once my terror dissipated somewhat I was anxious to revive the experience—but the book proved to have been returned to another branch, and I had no idea how to retrieve it, nor even the author's name. Not until I bought a copy of M. R. James's collected ghost stories did I recognise the episodes in "The Residence at Whitminster," one of his most complex narratives. His reticent method took some years to take root in my writing, but flourished once it did.

For years my library borrowings built up my view of the field. On the one hand, I feasted on Cynthia Asquith's second and third *Ghost Books*, relishing the contents in proportion to the dread the contents offered. The perennial Dorothy L. Sayers books—*Great Short Stories of Detection, Mystery and Horror*—also came my way. I think all these books set out to make a case for the literary validity of our field, and I'm inclined to believe Sayers was bidding to counteract the image Christine Campbell Thomson ("From the first, I set myself against 'literature'") had perpetrated with her *Not at Night* books. Anthologies by Derleth and Conklin introduced me to the pulps and the fifties digests they became, though we may observe the editors selected distinguished contributions, able to hold their own against work more respectably published. It's worth noting that despite using quite a few stories from *Weird Tales*, Derleth's choices almost never overlap with Thomson, even in his horror anthologies (not that the library stocked those or hers), perhaps because she mainly drew on the inferior first years of the publication. A couple of books I've subsequently been involved in celebrated his style of title: *The Far Reaches of Fear* (*Superhorror* retitled for paperback) and in particular *The Watchers and Other Wakeful Things*, a title I would like to think he might himself have approved if not invented for that collection of his tales.

I'm sure some of these library finds settled into whichever part of my mind produces fiction—in some cases settled decades deep. Perhaps Agatha Christie's unobtrusive linguistic dexterity and narrative ingenuity found a niche as well; she was one of my mother's favourite writers, and my recent reappraisal of her work prompted me to write a combined tribute and critique, *The Village Killings*. Back in my early years, I wrote a novella (*Dogs in the Stratosphere*) in clumsy emulation of *City*, Clifford Simak's canine science fiction novel. To its and our benefit, it was lost long ago and must remain a legend, or at least as much of one as it deserves.

Elsewhere I've described how encountering Herman Melville's "Bartleby" in John Keir Cross's *Best Horror Stories* when I was eleven and finding its inclusion somehow appropriate expanded my sense of the breadth of the field. To a progressive extent the quality of my reading left me critical of lesser stuff, but I still read it, hungry for horror as I was (though dread would do), and so I devoured issues of the new British magazine *Phantom* in the hope of something stronger than the demurely spectral and less wormy with clichés than I recognised most of the contents were. Alas, this awareness failed to prevent my committing many such offenses in my ramshackle first collection, *Ghostly Tales*. The magazine improved once it began to reprint choice material from *Weird Tales*, not least by Everil Worrell: her magnificently loopy fantasy "The Hollow Moon" and the earlier vampire story, "The Canal" (the original version, not the one substantially rewritten—presumably by Worrell—for Derleth's *Sleeping and the Dead*). Perhaps some of her extravagance insinuated itself into my rickety early stuff.

Several anthologies helped extend my concept of the field in the way "Bartleby" had. To an extent Wise and Fraser's *Great Tales of Terror and the Supernatural* did. I gradually came to agree that Hemingway's "The Killers" belonged in the first category. To begin with its inimitable spareness kept its chill out of my reach, but I felt compelled to return for more than one reread. By contrast, I've never understood what Hardy's "The Three Strangers" was doing in there: a good yarn, but where's the terror? Whit and Hallie Burnett's *19 Tales of Terror* offered similar conundrums in the shape of tales by Flann O'Brien and Karen Blixen (fine work, certainly) but impressed me with the way a shift of perspective could render a theme fearful; in "Paul's Tale" Mary Norton does so by giving us a glimpse of a Borrower through the eyes of a nervous adult. It's an enterprising anthology—many of the stories seem never to have been reprinted since—and takes insanity as its central theme, or at any rate extremes of mental experience. Whereas many of the contributors weren't associated with our field, Don Congdon's *Stories for the Dead of Night* included familiar names (and overlapped the Burnetts with just one tale, "The Two Bottles of Relish," dropping the definite article en route). While the Burnetts only had a tale in which a fellow imagines he's Poe, Congdon put Edgar in. Among the contributions that affected me profoundly were Elizabeth Bowen's "The Demon Lover," evoking London after the blitz; Edith Wharton's oppressively disturbing "A Journey"; Gwyn Jones's claustrophobic descent into darkness "The Pit." You may find traces of all these in my stuff, but the shock of "Miss Gentilbelle"—Charles Beaumont's first published story—was inimitable.

Soon I set out to embrace the mainstream in my reading. In my mid-teens and for some years after I mainly read outside my field. While I'd previously ventured there, now it became my preferred territory, but I still valued disquiet above all. There was plenty to be had: Pinkie's activities and his view of the world in *Brighton Rock*, Scobie's fate in *The Heart of the Matter*, the consul's end in *Under the Volcano* (perhaps an influence on *Los Olvidados*, which was certainly an influence on me), the paranoia that peers through the narrative interstices of *Jealousy* (*La Jalousie*, a pun beyond translating), the vision of a terrifying afterlife I believe the third volume of Beckett's trilogy gives us and the disquieting variation Golding conveys in *Pincher Martin*, the schizoid saga of *I Hear Voices* that feels constantly poised to tip into nightmare, the oppressive vividness of the mundane in *Nausea* (recalling comparable transformations in de Maupassant), *Lolita*'s disconcerting shifts of tone and the fate of Krug's son in *Bend Sinister*, rendered all the more horrific by the detached clinical language that describes it . . . I hardly needed any of these to convince me that unease and stronger versions of it were at large in the mainstream, a perception that encouraged me to write fiction that sometimes overlapped the categories. I brought back what I'd learned outside my field and followed its lead where I could. The late David Drake used to say his work was the sum of everything he'd read. I increasingly suspect the same is true of mine.

The Hollowing of Hatred

Géza A. G. Reilly

SCOTT R. JONES. *Drill*. Petaluma, CA: Worde Horde, 2024. 256 pp. $19.99 tpb. ISBN: 9781956252095.

What does hatred do to someone? What effect does it have to hate something so completely, so utterly, that the very fabric of one's being is warped by the strength of that hatred? Might hating someone or something so completely, so purely, hollow us out in a way, removing all that makes us fine and noble and replacing it with an emptiness never to be filled?

Is hatred an absence? Or is it a drill that leaves an absence in its wake?

Drill, by Scott R. Jones, is a brilliant exercise in High Weirdness that is, at the same time, intensely annoying. I say that because the protagonist of *Drill* is . . . Scott R. Jones, mailman, sorcerer, and author of weird fiction. It would be preposterous to think of *Drill* as autobiography, but at the same time I had to stop myself repeatedly while reading and mutter "wait, no, this can't be real" under my breath. Authorial inserts are nothing new, of course, but in *Drill* so much is bound up in Scott R. Jones as a person that I honestly found it difficult to keep track of where the author ended and the eponymous character stepped in. That all served to make the read a difficult one, and I ultimately found it next to impossible to determine whether Jones was trying to convey something about his own life, a gripping fictional narrative, or something in between.

Which isn't to say that *Drill* is unsatisfying. It absolutely is a gripping, enjoyable . . . novel? Perhaps "screed" would be better. I find it difficult to think of *Drill* as a novel because of, well, the aforementioned autobiographical qualities, but also because there isn't really much of plot here to speak of. In *Drill* we meet Scott R. Jones, who hates his father for shunning him after Jones breaks from the Jehovah's Witnesses.

Further, Jones hates the Jehovah's Witnesses and their god, and . . . that's largely the bulk of the book. Jones, the author, spends so much time focusing on Jones, the character, stoking the fires of his hatred toward these three targets that not much else gets center-stage.

Sure, there's the Drill itself. Did I mention the Drill? The Drill is a metaphysical machine digging its way through the superstructure of the body of God, which is the universe, in an unending quest to reach one of God's vital organs and, by doing so, displace all the *other* Drills from *other* realities and lock *this* reality in as the one true reality. Through his workings as a sorcerer (most notably his unceasing harassment of his father as part of his magical Great Work), Jones-the-character hooks up with the crew of the Drill to kill the god of the Jehovah's Witnesses (not necessarily the capital-G God of the Christian Bible, but Jones gets fuzzy in the details there). Doing so would finally bring his hatred to a climax, obliterating what is most loathed in an effort at something that might be healing and something that might be self-annihilation. It would also, conveniently, provide the sappers running the Drill with the explosive energy they need to further their work.

So . . . *Drill* is weird. Unabashedly so. It is packed with High Weirdness in a way that I, personally, haven't seen in many years. And Jones (the author, but possibly the character, too) revels in that High Weirdness. There are so many cultural touchstones here that certain kinds of readers will be enthralled. From obvious references to the Cthulhu Mythos (both Jones-as-author and Jones-as-character are high priests of a Cthulhu cult draped with Chaos Magick), to working in the Angry Fist of JVHV1 from the Church of the Subgenius, to a character based on the life and writing of Douglas Rushkoff, to blink-and-you've-missed-it quotations from the philosophy of Eugene Thacker, *Drill* luxuriates in a particular kind of literary bath that few texts are willing to dip their toes into. On that level, and as a devotee of High Weirdness, I can thoroughly recommend *Drill*. Buy it for yourself, buy it for your grandmother, buy it for your infant's crib.

Underneath that weirdness, though, underneath all that

scorn-filled screed, is something deeper. Something that doesn't really have to be ironically dug out. As I suggested at the outset of this review, I came away from *Drill* thinking about the effects hatred has on the individual. Those effects aren't rosy, of course, but perhaps it goes deeper than that. Is hatred the thing that hollows? Does it destroy the best within the one who hates? Jones-the-character admits at several points that he is *not* the hero of this book—stripped of all sorcerous pretense, his actions are nothing more than a series of unrelenting attacks on an old man who is, at the end of the day, completely harmless. If that is the case, then what would it result if he were to succeed in his quest to tear down that old man, to destroy the church to which he belongs, or to murder the god he worships? Jones's triumph would leave behind the shattered remains of a person who has been stripped of everything he once thought good and holy, certainly, but . . . what would remain of Jones himself after that?

Drill is a fascinating piece of work. I haven't read much, if any, of Jones's writing before coming across this book, but I know for sure that I'll be searching out more of what he's produced in the near future. There aren't that many . . . novels? screeds? out there that gave me as much joy in the jaw-dropping indulgence in High Weirdness that this one has, just as there aren't many that made me truly sit and think about something as common, and as petty, as the real effects of hatred upon the target and the source alike when it is loosed upon the world. I'll say this now: *Drill* is absolutely not for everyone. It is, however, a rarity among its contemporaries. It has something to say, and it drinks in rarified air on its path to saying it. If the reader is tripped up by the mixture of truth and fiction, by metaphor and certainty, by weirdness and prosaic reality, it is only because there is something profound to be explored within those twists and turns.

Driven by suffering the Drill may be, but there is always the chance that its turning might reveal gold.

Traducteur pour Le Fantastique: Brian Stableford, 1948–2024

The joey Zone

Almost a quarter of a century ago, it was *The Fin de Millénaire*. There were tales of Atlantis. Of Carnival and plague and bat-winged batrachians. Of a harpy queen experiencing ecstasy in a death that "need not end desire." They were related in a style similar to accounts of a lost Hyperborea or prophecies of a dying earth to come and it was a pleasurable geas to illustrate them. A chapbook of saffron enwrapped these *Fables and Fantasies* for Necronomicon Press in 1996. Brian Stableford was their author.

Necronomicon Press (1996), art by The joey Zone.

On February 24th of this year, Brian Stableford died, age seventy-five.

A Frenchman could look at his bibliography and pronounce it *formidable*. He had written more than seventy of his own novels as well as shorter fictions. But besides this, much of his later career was devoted to bringing nearly 380 translations of French novels and stories (some dating back to the seventeenth century) into English, with fifteen more upcoming titles from publishers Snuggly Books and Black Coat Press.

In 1985, Stableford won the Eaton Award for *Scientific Romance in Britain: 1890–1950*. It was "the only academic book I ever managed to publish . . . [and] only sold 157 copies," Stableford stated. "I became very interested in . . . comparisons and contrasts between [British & American fictions] and the early evolution of European traditions."

At ConFuse (19)91 he had the following to say about an early foray into a Trans-Channel anthology, *The Dedalus Book of Decadence: Moral Ruins*, published in 1990: "[The publishers said] We have put this book in our catalogue and now it is four weeks to go." When asked to make deadline, Stableford said, "Well, yes, I will do my best. . . . I had to do it myself which was difficult [as translations were needed] because I don't speak French. But now I read French tolerably well. There are dictionaries, you know." Brian gifted me a copy—not for review but because I evinced a shared comfort found in this literary milieu en général. This kindness gave introductions to the work of Jean Lorrain (a votive candle now tended under the beringed fierceness of Gandara's portrait in my aesthetic pantheon); supernaturally tinged erotica penned by Remy de Gourmont, who hid from sight due to Lupus; and Catulle Mendès, whose novel *Mephistophela* (1890) boasts passages of great hallucinatory diabolism.

Also sent gratis was the follow-up to this collection, *The Second Dedalus Book of Decadence: The Black Feast* (1992). It is blessed with one of the most gorgeous covers ever assigned to a paperback publication, with matte gold surrounded title and a reproduction of Gustave Moreau's *The Apparition* (1874/1876). In this volume I first read the work of Marcel Schwob (key collection by him being *The King in The Golden Mask* [1892]) and Anatole France, with "Saint Satyr," an excerpt from *The Well of St. Clare* (1895). This and a handful of other works by France were superbly illustrated by Frank C. Papé for The Bodley Head in the 1920s.

The same year I received these, 1999, Stableford won the Pilgrim Award, given by the Science Fiction Research Association for a lifetime achievement in science fiction criticism. As to research, he labeled himself "a confirmed antiquarian, fascinated by the thankless task of tracing . . . ideas through literary history."

"It is easy to get obsessive about the historical and bibliographical things. When you find, in some sort of forgotten corner . . . a fact that nobody else knew or . . . find a book nobody else have ever heard of, this comes to seem like a great discovery . . . I do take terrible delight in discovering authors that nobody else have ever heard of and writing critical articles about them. I know that the definite critical articles only get read by three people but even so there is a sense in that once they are on the record they are there." Written akin to some *Dead Reckonings* contributor . . .

In the November 2011 issue of *Locus,* Stableford vowed to "try to [translate more works] as thoroughly as I can before blindness sets in or the grim reaper comes knocking." Seven years after that, the collection *Decadence and Symbolism: A Showcase Anthology,* published by Snuggly Books, continued this promise. A wider aesthetic was previewed by the cover reproduction of Paul Signac's pointillist *Portrait of Félix Fénéon* (1890), anarchist and feuillettoniste. Two new introductions were made to me: Jane de la Vaudère, apparently frequenting the same ensanguined jardins as Octave Mirbeau yet not living as long; and Henri de Régnier, whose translated collection of dark Fae, *A Surfeit of Mirrors,* was proffered by Black Coat Press in 2012.

A standout selection was Jean Lorrain's "The Toad (Le Crapaud)" (1895), the title's subject an embodiment of the decadent's revulsion to Nature, both in general and in oneself: "It was, moreover, a monstrously large toad, whose like I have never seen since: a magician toad, at least a hundred years old, half-gnome, half-beast of the Sabbat; one of those gold-crowned toads that one hears of in folktales, set to watch over hidden treasures in ruined cities with a deadly nightshade flower beneath its left foot, nourishing itself on human blood."

Stableford was then not merely a translator *of,* but *for* the material, serving to set the imagery as brilliantly as possible, craftsmanship only found in the rarest *bijoux superlatifs.* There remain so many writers whose work curated by him this reviewer needs to discover! *The Vermilion Book of Occult Fiction* (2022) and *The Alabaster Book of Occult Fiction* (2023), both published by Snuggly Books, for example, are two dark mirror images of Andrew Lang's rainbow-hued collections of fairy tales from the late nineteenth century.

Mike Hoffmann has done many covers for Stableford including this anthology published by Black Coat Press.

It is in this resurrection of imaginations beyond his own that Brian Stableford has kept whole decades alive. "Once they are on the record they are there." The stardust left in the tail of his comet will remain visible to discerning eyes for years to come—What is remembered, lives.

Sources

locusmag.com/2011/11/spotlight-on-brian-stableford-translator-and-author/

www.blackgate.com/2024/02/28/brian-stableford-july-25-1948-february-24-2024/

www.infinityplus.co.uk/nonfiction/intbs06.htm

www.lysator.liu.se/lsff/mb-nr25/Interview_with_Brian_Stableford.html

Ligotti and the Tradition of Wishful Selfhood

Katherine Kerestman

> "The greatest horror is the loss of identity."
> —H. P. Lovecraft, "Through the Gates of the Silver Key"

I. Selfhood in Horror

To cease to exist. Not only to die and survive in some incorporeal form. Not only to sleep until the resurrection. Not merely to be recycled into a new person or other creature. But to cease being. This is the ultimate horror.

Whether one accepts Descartes's oft-reiterated notion that "I think, therefore I am" or not, one must surely acknowledge that, for us sentient beings, at least, the existence of a Self and the existence of thought are inseparable phenomena, whatever the relationship between Self and thought may be. When attempting to define or classify "Self," a person thinks about what he or she is; and, by thinking, a person delineates or draws the boundaries between his or her Self and all that which is not part of that Self. It is generally accepted that (1) a Self exists for each one of us; (2) that the raw material of Self is not brought into being out of nothingness by the Self; and (3) that a person's Self, once existing, is developed by oneself, notwithstanding great influence by that which is outside the Self.

A more frightening concept, even, than the destruction of an existing Self, also known as Identity, is the possibility that there is no such thing as self, only an "illusion of identity" (Lovecraft 904). In "Through the Gates of the Silver Key," Randolph Carter is many Randolph Carters and is only a part or "fragment now facing the PRESENCE in the limitless abyss" (Lovecraft 905). Perhaps the boundaries we have defined, or set up, around the Self are fluid, mutable, or even nonexistent. Lovecraft's funhouse mirror room concept of Self distorted and multiplied is reiterated in *Twin Peaks* and in the works of Ligotti (and many other tales of horror that may not be discussed in this limited space). The loss of one's Self is, in fact, the greatest horror of them all, yet is often overlooked when presented with immediate danger to life and limb.

The unity of effect of a horror story—that confluence of elements which creates the reader's experience of the horrific—is attained through skillful interplay of language (vocabulary, idiom, imagery), characters, plot, and atmosphere, with just enough realism to make the imaginary immediate and visceral. Together, these elements lead up to a threat. The threat may include injury or loss to oneself or others. The threat may be death, defined as the dissolution of the physical container that houses the Self (i.e., the body—and yet, is the body really separate from the Self?). It may be the destruction of society—the forest that hears the tree/the Self fall and, hearing, provides objective evidence of the existence of said tree/the Self—which is threatened. Perhaps it is the possible complete annihilation of the Self, that which is separate from all else, which looms.

Caught up in the situational danger of the injury or the death of a sympathetic character, whom the author has endowed with a delineated Self or Identity, the reader may overlook the greater peril of the utter non-existence of that character—which gives certain works an especial poignancy. Many casual readers, for instance, in anticipation of how the story will end and fascinated by the blood-sucking, overlook the central theme of *Dracula:* the threat to the integrity of Self. In Stoker's masterwork, victory is not in staking a vampire or saving lives but in wresting the mastery, or control, of Self from outside influences. Dracula's mesmeric and seductive qualities are only the foremost of the many threats to a sovereign Self.

It seems to me that the precarious nature of Selfhood is a continuing theme in all great horror; as another example, I will refer to one of my favorite stories, *Twin Peaks* (1990–1991, 2017). Laura is the center of *Twin Peaks*, according to the Log Lady, and yet, great pains are taken to demonstrate that there is no center—and also no beginning or end. There are no boundaries (from texts to people and places), for Laura is defined by many, and conflicting, terms by a society that also invades her. Aliens abduct characters. Prehistoric cave paintings depict current phenomena and events. Dimensions overlap and blend. Persons are multiple personalities and doppelgängers; that is to say, persons are not discrete but are fluid, interpersonal entities. Intertextuality melds all perceptions of reality into one kaleidoscopic cosmos, a cosmic maelstrom in which an infinite number of consciousnesses swirl and commingle.

Even H. P. Lovecraft, whose cosmic fear is most often focused, like his telescope, on the spaces between the stars, must confront the idea of his own Self facing annihilation. In a letter to Maurice W. Moe, Lovecraft writes, "Nothing in heaven or earth is so important to the man of spirit and imagination as the inviolate integrity of his cerebral life—his sense of utter integration and defiant independence as a proud, lone entity face-to-face with the illimitable cosmos. And if he be the general temperament which usually goes with such a mental makeup, he will too be apt to consider a haughty celibacy any great price to pay for this ethereal inviolateness" (*Lord of a Visible World* 207). He describes his attitude in heroic terms as if he were climbing Mount Everest rather than courageously confronting the infinite abyss: "I refer to the aesthetic crystallisation of that burning & inextinguishable feeling of wonder & oppression which the sensitive imagination experiences upon scaling itself & its restrictions against the vast & provocative abyss of the unknown. This has always been the chief emotion in my psychology" (quoted in Joshi, *I Am Providence* 779). Yet, in all of the stories he wrote after "The Shadow over Innsmouth" (1931), the focus of his horror shifts from the malevolent abyss to the violated Self. Devastated by the rejection of *At the Mountains of Madness* and suspecting that his intestinal illness was terminal, Lovecraft also had to consider the possibility that his Self has never existed independently at all. In "Through the Gates of the Silver Key," for instance, Lovecraft zeroes in on "the horror of destroyed individuality" (Lovecraft 903) and the "illusion of identity" (904), while Carter becomes "a fragment now facing the PRESENCE in the limitless abyss" (905). So that his point is not missed, Lovecraft spells it plainly:

No death, no doom, no anguish can arouse the surpassing despair which flows from a loss of *identity*. Merging with nothingness is peaceful oblivion; but to be aware of existence and yet to know that one is no longer a definite being distinguished form other beings—that one no longer has a *self*—that is the nameless summit of agony and dread. (902)

The protagonist of "The Shadow out of Time" finds that he is only a *projection* of another entity. The identity of Charles Dexter Ward is subsumed by his more powerful forebear. Henry Wentworth Akeley, of "The Whisperer in the Darkness," is no more than a brain in a jar. Faced with his own obliteration, Lovecraft's tone becomes brooding, subdued, and melancholy. He is no longer the exuberant and florid story teller he was. He writes lengthy expository passages and philosophical disquisitions about alien societies and the meaning of Selfhood, for the ultimate horror lies in his own gradual discovery of the abominable secret that he is no more than his own youthful illusions that his independent Self has never existed at all.

II. Ligotti in the Tradition of Wishful Selfhood

I have only recently discovered Thomas Ligotti, having purchased three of his books as souvenirs of a trip to Portland, Oregon, in which strange country I was wandering like a lost soul in the melancholy aftermath of the H. P. Lovecraft Film Festival and the departure of my Lovecraftian friends. Curious to learn what all the fuss was about, I read his books—and it came as no surprise that the question of Identity is as predominant a theme for Ligotti as other prominent horror writers. For Ligotti also, Self is an illusion. Not only is the individual invaded by terrestrial forces, particularly the machinery of capitalism and social pressure to conformity, but people are, for all their hubris, merely puppets manipulated by a hostile cosmos who only think they have free will.

In *The Conspiracy against the Human Race*, Ligotti writes that in the worlds of Lovecraft terrible entities pull the strings: "Azathoth the Blind Idiot God, Nyarlathothep the Crawling Chaos, Cthulhu the Dead Dreamer: These are some of the entities that symbolize the Lovecraftian universe as a place without sense, meaning, or value" (*Conspiracy* 111). In Ligotti (as in *Dracula* and *Twin Peaks*), characters are the unwitting pawns of higher forces and villains are the representatives of a malevolent cosmos at large. Dominio, in *My Work Is Not Yet Done*, plots to seize control of his world (which has been working relentlessly to grind him into a cog in the Machine), to which end he formulates and deploys workplace revenge fantasies. Just as he begins to relish his personal power, he discovers that all along both he and his enemies have been the pawns of dark, alien entities. This set-up posits the questions of whether there are any beneficent cosmic forces and, if so, why they allow the horrors to be perpetrated upon a puppet-people.

The tales collected in *Songs of a Dead Dreamer* and *Grimscribe* explore the concepts of consciousness, objective reality, and discrete selfhood. The prose is quite variable in tone, even beautiful at times. I don't like these stories because they are too dirty, despicable, and ugly for my taste. (While I appreciate the work of Joyce Carol Oates, I can take her stories only in small doses, for the same reason.) Despite the moments of beauty, I feel that generally the prose is flat and painfully plain, not effervescent nor spine-tingly. Some of his vocabulary is pompous, rather than evocative of dark dimensions and horrid things. To illustrate the concept that we are all puppets manipulated by a maleficent puppeteer (an enigmatic cosmos), Ligotti employs the imagery of mannequins. He uses mannequins over and over. Reading the things people do to mannequins and to each other is brutal. In a surreal merging of the here and now with alternate realities, it is as if Ligotti tried to be Lovecraft or Bradbury in his depiction of cosmic horror and failed.

My Work Is Not Yet Done, however, is different. It is superb. I began reading it at work (I know . . .) and, by the time I went to bed that evening, I knew that I would need to finish reading it with a drink in my hand because it was so unsettling. Gone is the pseudo-sophisticated diction. Gone is the repetitive mannequin imagery that goes nowhere. I finished reading it at a restaurant the next day, where I broke my fast with toast and a Mimosa to serve as an anaesthetic. When I got home, I was still too agitated by my reading to remain there, so I went to the library to work. I needed desperately to subsume my pain in something, to release my tension. Eventually, I felt subdued. Such is the power of a well-written piece of literature to evoke emotion.

My Work Is Not Yet Done describes the pain of those who feel oppressed and ground up by their workplaces, or the pain of the victims of bullies in other environments. It is the pain of the outsider, the hunted, the raped. It is the first-person narrative of a man who works in a cubicle; who comes up with a groundbreaking idea; who is emotionally, physically, and professionally abused by his co-workers and managers; and who plots elaborate scenarios of revenge. In the midst of playing out his fantasies Dominio learns that both he and his enemies are puppets whose strings are managed by monstrous entities whose motives are unfathomable to our species. At that point the game is up, but Dominio is unwilling to concede the idea of Selfhood: "There is nothing left to save if ever there was anything . . . if ever there could be. All we desire (in all our bitterness) is to go to ruin *in our own way*—with a little style and a lot of noise" (176). Reading this powerful text, I was obliged to confront that same darkness within myself, the darkness that is omnipresent in existence and not only in select individuals, places, or circumstances: "We—all of us—are the darkness that dreams are made on" (132). My past experiences at the hands of bullies (inside and outside of the workplace) rose to the surface. All is darkness, only—tragically—we are able to imagine more. This book upset my equilibrium.

The third book I brought home from witch-haunted Portland is *The Conspiracy against the Human Race*. This nonfiction work puts forth Ligotti's philosophy of pessimistic existential horror in terms of its historical development and its place in literature and society in general. Simply stated, it would have been better not to have been born. Self-conscious existence is a tragedy because we are aware of our finiteness and suffer from our awareness of it, as well as from the awareness that we are doomed to suffer in more ways than one. I find all these ideas intriguing, and probably true; but I do not like the puppet metaphor of many of his stories. Apart from its overuse throughout these pages, it implies that Some Thing is pulling our strings, not merely a materialist determinism, a roll of DNA and subatomic dice. I'm not sure I can wrap my mind around a string-puller in real life. In *Conspiracy*, Ligotti discusses at length various philosophers who advocate eschewing reproduction for the good of the species; that is, to prevent future people from suffering the way we do. Ligotti offers one coping mechanism available to us all, distraction with our hobbies; unfortunately, an awareness that one's interests are biologically predetermined can siphon the joy out of them, for we can no longer claim to be individual or unique. "What is most uncanny about the self is that no one has yet been able to present the least evidence of it" (88).

Works Cited

Joshi, S. T. *I Am Providence: The Life and Times of H. P. Lovecraft*. New York: Hippocampus Press, 2010.

Ligotti, Thomas. *Songs of a Dead Dreamer and Grimscribe*. New York: Penguin, 2015.

———. *My Work Is Not Yet Done*. 2002. New York: Random House, 2009.

———. *The Conspiracy against the Human Race*. 2010. New York: Penguin, 2018.

Lovecraft, H. P. *The Complete Fiction*. New York: Barnes & Noble, 2011.

———. *Lord of a Visible World: An Autobiography in Letters*. Ed. S. T. Joshi and David E. Schultz. 2000. New York: Hippocampus Press, 2019.

Midsummer Shamblings: NecronomiCon Providence et al.

Darrell Schweitzer

I will start this on a personal note by saying that I am damned glad I didn't have to do this year's NecronomiCon Providence in a wheelchair. It could have happened. It came very close to happening.

The summer convention season was heavy. I started out with NECon, a.k.a. Camp NECon, a.k.a. Northeast Regional Fantasy Convention (a name no one uses), July 18–21. This has traditionally been held in Rhode Island, usually on or adjoining the Roger Williams University campus, but in the last couple of years had switched to Lowell, Massachusetts. This year it moved to very nice facilities on the St. Anselm College campus near Manchester, New Hampshire. (The joke is that if we keep moving northward like that, we will be at the North Pole before long.) There were some growing pains as we settled in. I got all the way to the campus by myself, without using a GPS (sometimes asking directions of locals who had never heard of the place), but it was only when I was on the campus itself, circling for half an hour in the dark, that I had to call the chairman's emergency number for rescue and tell him what building I was in front of so he could come and get me. It all made a lot more sense the following morning by daylight. St. Anselm's is a Catholic college, so there were crucifixes everywhere. I remarked this made us free from vampires for the weekend. I understand that the priests or monks who ran the place were quite cool with the idea of hosting a horror writers' con. A couple of them attended the program.

It is hard to describe what NECon means to outsiders. Not that it is clannish or unwelcoming to newbies. Far from it. But it also has aspects of a family reunion. It is small enough that everybody knows everybody, and longtime NEConners regard one another as far more than just convention acquaintances. This year was the forty-second NECon. I was not sure if I was the only person present who had attended the first one, but we had our share of old-timers. NECon has a Hall of Fame, into which I was inducted in 2014. I am one of the few Hall of Famers who was never a guest of honor. I guess they just couldn't get rid of me. I have been a panelist for most of those forty-two years, became a Legend (another NECon ranking) in 1998, have contributed to most of the NECon books, collected medals in the NECon Olympics (for throwing darts; arguably cheating by doing it sober), and so on. NECon is very much an affair of fun and games, but it also has good programming and you can meet and talk to very interesting writers. It is the kind of place where, some years back, I was able to take Jonathan Carroll aside for a couple hours and do a really good interview with him. This year I met S. A. Cosby, who is a thriller writer from the South. I realized I had heard of him before. I heard him interviewed on NPR. They were giving out copies of his *All the Sinners Bleed* in the goodie bags, so I intend to make his further acquaintance.

But to get back to the narrative thread that involves wheelchairs. I went to NECon as a dealer. I always do. I can usually make about enough to pay for my presence there. (NECon membership comes with room and board. You eat in the cafeteria. You sleep in dorms.) I LIFTED A LOT OF HEAVY BOXES. I even went home heavier than I came, when one generous fellow gave me several crates of his unsold stock.

The following weekend, July 26–28, I was at Confluence, which is a pleasant little science fiction convention in the Pittsburgh area that I switched to when the once-welcoming Readercon decided to do demographic purges. For me, from Philadelphia, Pittsburgh is about as far away as Boston. I could go as readily to one as another. I even figured out a way to evade the PA Turnpike toll (which would be about $100 each way), in a dramatically scenic route that takes me over the Appalachians (rather than under them; no tunnels) and through that remote and virtually uninhabited northwestern corner of Pennsylvania where there are no doubt more sasquatches than people, and, very likely, my eldritch village of Chorazin, about which I have written much, is to be found.

And I LIFTED A LOT OF HEAVY BOXES. This time it caught up with me. Right as the dealers' room closed on Sunday I innocently stood up from a chair and felt a disk slipping in my lower back. This has happened before. I knew perfectly well what it was. I sat right down and tried to relax, but this did me no good. People helped me load up. Someone lent me a back brace during the process. I made my way home, almost nine hours, not uncomfortable when actually seated, but emerging from my car by hanging on the door and hauling myself up, and staggering in to rest stops.

There is no respite for the wicked. Three days later I was due to go right back to the Pittsburgh area for the grand and glorious Pulpfest (August 1–4), but by Tuesday I was in such bad shape I tried to cancel. The hotel told me I couldn't do that without being charged. But they did offer me a wheelchair. So I paused for a minute, then said I would come. I alerted the con people that I was going to need help. I will neither confirm nor deny (caution: Star Trek reference coming up) that the Grand Nagus of the Ferengi appeared to me in a vision and said, "Go, make a profit." I did say to one of the hotel people that I was glad I came because I could have been just as uncomfortable at home and made a lot less money. People were very supportive and helpful. I had to tell many of them that, no, this was not the new me, just the temporary me, that I was not disabled, merely inconvenienced. Selling books must have therapeutic value, because by the end of the weekend I was able to get up and walk with the aid of a cane, even help lift a few of those boxes as we loaded out. (But the Grand Nagus did suggest using more, smaller boxes in the future, not the big fifty-pounders.)

What is particularly of interest to *Dead Reckonings* readers is that Pulpfest and its larger cousin, Windy City Pulp Con, which is near Chicago, are the last great antiquarian book events you will find in the convention circuit. Yes, the emphasis is on pulp magazines. The excellent programming consisted of sideshow presentations about *Black Mask,* the Spicy pulps, dinosaurs in pulp art, etc. It was also a chance to meet some colleagues and even do a little business. But the main attraction was a huckster room large enough to land a small plane in, and the Saturday night auction. This is where collections go when old fans die. This is where you can still find Arkham House and other specialty-press books, and rare periodicals of all sorts (including fanzines from the 1940s). A few of the prices are preposterous. Somebody had that "iconic" 1932 Bat Girl issue of *Weird Tales* for (I think it was) $12,000; but that item really does command a lot these days. One actually sold in the auction for $4000. But there were also many reasonably priced bargains, including a few I could scarf up cheaply either for upgrading my own collection or for resale on eBay. I found a pile of 1930s *Astounding*s for $10 apiece. When I kick the bucket, I'd like there to be a Schweitzer Estate Auction at Pulpfest. It is a way to keep your treasures within the community.

Now, having once more braved the sasquatches and mountainous inclines (the only place I have ever seen a runaway truck lane, between State College and Harrisburg), I got to rest for one whole week, slowly unloading and reloading the car for NecronomiCon Providence (August 15–18), which is held every two years, in (you guessed it) Providence, Rhode Island. Fortunately there were ample Minions available (they were uniform T-shirts that say MINION) to help me with all those big, heavy boxes. I was just using a cane by this point. I used to conduct walking tours of Lovecraftian sites in Providence, but, at a few days short of seventy-two, I declared myself retired as a tour guide and concentrated on the book-hustling. Sales at a NecronomiCon are whole orders of magnitude greater than anywhere else. I had only one table, right next to Hippocampus Press, so we could support each other when somebody was called away to be on a panel. I mostly sold my own books, my Lovecraftian anthologies, my Lovecraftian hymnals, etc., plus Wildside Press editions of Dunsany and Robert E. Howard. I signed an unbelievable amount of books that weekend. I had an informal autograph line going at my table at one point. I do believe that at NecronomiCon I am close to being an actual celebrity rather than a mere fixture.

NecronomiCon in its full glory is of course something not to be missed. It is the Worldcon of the Lovecraftian universe. People actually do come from all over the world to attend, about two to three thousand of them. For all Lovecraft may be politically incorrect in some circles (I understand they have removed the Lovecraft bust from the Providence Athenaeum; well, remove the Athenaeum from our tours), he is Providence's most famous son. I met a Frenchman a couple NecronomiCons ago, who said they asked him at the airport why he was going to Providence, not usually a city that attracts European tourists, his one-word answer was "Lovecraft."

Like a Worldcon, NecronomiCon is so spread out and diverse that you inevitably miss more than you can attend. There is an academic track, called the Armitage Symposium, in which learned papers are read. The best of these are published biannually by Hippocampus Press as *Lovecraftian Proceedings*. There are panels, readings, theatrical presentations, receptions, and more. One strong hint: When attending NecronomiCon, get to as many of the theatrical presentations as you can. They may be the marvelous radio plays performed live by the H. P. Lovecraft Historical Society (this year I managed to attend their version of "The Shunned House") or the equally marvelous M. R. James impersonations/recitals by Robert Lloyd Parry. This year also featured a dramatic reading of "Beyond the Wall of Sleep" performed by Andrew Leman (of HPLHS), with a musical soundtrack by Chris Bozzone (of Cadabra Records). Between my busy/exhausting huckstering activities and one exclusive off-site party on Saturday night, I didn't get to as much as I would have liked, but I tried. The art reception a few blocks away from the main hotels in the Providence Arcade (the oldest shopping center in Providence, possibly in America, which contains the Lovecraft Shop) had some impressive art but was sparsely attended because of the sudden and intense downpour that happened about then. Fortunately I was inside the building before the deluge began. Most of us looked at the art, then hung out with Andrew Leman, waiting for the rain to stop.

This year's guests of honor were s. j. bagley, Nadia Bulkin, Billy Martin, Mike Mason, Brandon O'Brien, Sheree Renée Thomas, and Jeff VanderMeer. Jeff was apparently ill and unable to attend, but his wife Ann VanderMeer was there. Some of the other weird fiction stars in attendance included Peter

Cannon, Michael Cisco, Frank Coffman, Will Murray, F. Brett Cox, Jeffrey Thomas, Jonathan Thomas, Peter Rawlik, Paul Di Filippo, Stephen Rainey, John Langan, Michael Dirda, Simon Strantzas, Kenneth Hite, Nicholas Kaufmann, Cody Goodfellow, Paul Tremblay, Errick Nunnally, Anya Martin, and many other names I do not recognize. Had I the miraculous ability to be in six places at once, I could have made the acquaintance of more of them. I was in a group reading with Jeffrey Thomas, Will Ludwigsen, and Henrik Möller. This last gentleman was unknown to me, but his work was impressive and I was glad to have learned of him.

NecronomiCon is fun, and an educational experience, and I strictly deny that I am in it for the money, although, as I mentioned, sales (for me at least) in the dealers' room ranged between the astronomical and the truly cosmic. I was pleased to see more books there this year. I think somebody read my previous report on NecronomiCon, of two years ago, right here in *Dead Reckonings*, in which I said there was a definite niche open for more book dealers. You can get all sorts of Lovecraftian gewgaws there, everything from an authentic replica of the Cthulhu idol walrus tusk worshipped by degenerate Eskimos in the HPLHS movie of *The Call of Cthulhu* to a Lovecraft bobblehead; but the literature has to be the core of it, so I was pleased to see at least three antiquarian booksellers there, with Arkham House, Ash-Tree Press, and other collectible and expensive tomes. A few things seemed overpriced. I think $100 for a 1950 *Weird Tales* is a bit optimistic, though $100 for a very nice 1937 issue with a Finlay cover perhaps is not. I hope these folks did well. If I may pass on a bit more of my commercial wisdom, I think there is still an open niche for somebody with more modestly priced weird fiction, if it is still possible to scour mundane bookstores for cheap Blackwood and Machen and bring that sort of thing to NecronomiCon at a reasonable markup. Much classic weird fiction consists of things younger readers have heard of but not seen, so someone could do well putting it in their hands at affordable prices. Yes, and if you need a copy of *The Outsider and Others,* you can find that too.

Panel topics are rich and varied. You get a sense of the

community from the appreciative panels about important members who are no longer with us. This year there were memorial panels about Joe Pulver, Joel Lane, and Wilum Hopfrog Pugmire. I was on one about Frank Belknap Long (with Peter Cannon, Derrick Hussey, and David Goodwin). We explored FBL's legacy. I told anecdotes and quoted forty-year-old conversations ("Frank told me that Lovecraft had marvelous physical strength and could flip the lid off a Coke bottle with his thumb—you don't get that in any of the biographies"), while Peter, who knew Long well, went into considerably greater detail. This panel actually got a bit melancholy as we moved on to Frank Long's precarious later life and fading career.

Another panel I was on concerned Hollow Earth theories, John Symmes and all that, and how they influenced fantasy fiction. I had to do my homework for that one. I was also on a panel on the small-press magazines of the past half-century or so, complete with slide presentations of the covers. This was one case where I felt like I was actually part of the history we were describing. (Because I was. "Ooh! I'm in that one!") Other topics (of panels I wasn't on) ranged from panels about Arthur Machen and Franz Kafka to "Transgressive Horror and Weird Fiction" (an obvious one for Billy Martin), the Canadian Weird, the influence of Herman Melville on weird fiction, Mythos Influence on Heavy Metal, The Biology of the Elder Things, Impossible Architecture in Weird Fiction, and many more. You get the idea. A veritable feast. All one needs is teleportation and bilocation and you could see most of it. You can also go on walking tours of Lovecraft's Providence, some of them conducted by Donovan Loucks, who is an expert on both Lovecraft and Providence history, and, quite candidly, more qualified than I to do this sort of thing. Yes, I know where the Shunned House is, but Donovan figured out where Joseph Curwen used to live.

There are also the extravganzas. Waterfire on Saturday night. This is something put on by the city of Providence itself, on a nearby river and canal. Boats, costumes, flashing lights, music. Some years ago they actually raised a 60-foot Cthulhu for a virgin sacrifice at one of these, but not so this year. Still, a spectacle. Saturday night climaxes with the Eldritch Ball, a major event for costumers and folks who dance.

And then there is the Cthulhu Prayer Breakfast on Sunday morning. The usual hotel breakfast—eggs, bacon, diced shoggoth—but blasphemous services immediately follow, presided over by the Reverend Cody Goodfellow and Scott R. Jones and accompanied by yours truly and what Cody refers to as the Amorphous Tabernacle Choir. (Elite Gold Key members of the convention, in cultist robes.) Yes, while I have never sung for my supper, I have indeed sung for my breakfast. This is the only convention where I receive compliments for my singing voice. I guess that's because I was holding the mic while leading the choir, so the audience heard me more clearly. We used my hymns, taken from the two Innsmouth Tabernacle Choir chapbooks, a selection of them printed up in special pamphlets for the convention and placed on every table so the congregation could join in. I admit that when we sang about the Big Guy "We will raise him up / we will raise him up / we will raise him up upon the last day," I felt I was straining. What must have impressed them was my soulful crooning of "What a Friend We Have in Dagon."

Everything! Fun! Fellowship! Scholarship. A bit of gibbering madness, if in moderation. My thanks as always to Niels Hobbs, Anthony Teth, Ken Heard, and all the good folks who work so hard to make these events happen. I would not miss one of these for anything. To tell the truth, the reason I didn't go to the doctor after my back injury at Confluence was that I was afraid he was going to tell me not to go to Providence, and I was going to go to Providence. Moving back and forth between buildings and crossing streets, and getting to the twenty-second floor of the Biltmore for the prayer breakfast might have been a problem if I'd been in a wheelchair, but I would have done it if I had to.

I would have gritted my tentacles and soldiered on. We Lovecraftians are made of stern stuff. Eldritch wonder calls.

The Four-Fifteen Express

Amelia B. Edwards

The events which I am about to relate took place between nine and ten years ago. Sebastopol had fallen in the early spring, the peace of Paris had been concluded since March, our commercial relations with the Russian empire were but recently renewed; and I, returning home after my first northward journey since the war, was well pleased with the prospect of spending the month of December under the hospitable and thoroughly English roof of my excellent friend, Jonathan Jelf, Esq., of Dumbleton Manor, Clayborough, East Anglia. Travelling in the interests of the well-known firm in which it is my lot to be a junior partner, I had been called upon to visit not only the capitals of Russia and Poland, but had found it also necessary to pass some weeks among the trading ports of the Baltic; whence it came that the year was already far spent before I again set foot on English soil, and that, instead of shooting pheasants with him, as I had hoped, in October, I came to be my friend's guest during the more genial Christmastide.

My voyage over, and a few days given up to business in Liverpool and London, I hastened down to Clayborough with all the delight of a schoolboy whose holidays are at hand. My way lay by the Great East Anglian line as far as Clayborough station, where I was to be met by one of the Dumbleton carriages and conveyed across the remaining nine miles of country. It was a foggy afternoon, singularly warm for the 4th of December, and I had arranged to leave London by the 4:15 express. The early darkness of winter had already closed in; the lamps were lighted in the carriages; a clinging damp dimmed the windows, adhered to the door-handles, and pervaded all the atmosphere; while the gas-jets at the neighbouring bookstand diffused a luminous haze that only served to make the gloom of the terminus more visible. Having arrived some seven minutes before the starting of the train, and, by the connivance of the guard, taken sole possession of empty compartment, I lighted my travelling-lamp, made myself particularly snug, and settled down to the undisturbed enjoyment of a book and a cigar. Great, therefore, was my disappointment when, at the last moment, a gentleman came hurrying along the platform, glanced into my carriage, opened the locked door with a private key, a stepped in.

It struck me at the first glance that I had seen him before—a tall, spare man, thin-lipped, light-eyed, with an ungraceful stoop in the shoulders and scant gray hair worn somewhat long upon collar. He carried a light waterproof coat, an umbrella, and a large brown japanned deed-box, which last he placed under the seat. This done, he felt carefully in his breast-pocket, as if to make certain of the safety of his purse or pocketbook, laid his umbrella in the netting overhead, spread the waterproof across his knees, and exchanged his hat for a travelling-cap of some Scotch material. By this time the train was moving out of the station and into the faint gray of the wintry twilight beyond.

I now recognised my companion. I recognised him from the moment when he removed his hat and uncovered the lofty, furrowed, and somewhat narrow brow beneath. I had met him, as I distinctly remembered, some three years before, at the very house for which, in all probability, he was now bound, like myself. His name was Dwerrihouse, he was a lawyer by profession, and, if I was not greatly mistaken, was first cousin to the wife of my host. I knew also that he was a man eminently "well-to-do," both as regarded his professional and private means. The Jelfs entertained him with that sort of observant courtesy which falls to the lot of the rich relation, the children made much of him, and the old butler, albeit somewhat surly "to the general," treated him with deference. I thought, observing him by the vague mixture of lamplight and twilight, that Mrs. Jelf's cousin looked all the worse for the three years' wear and tear which had gone over his head since our last meeting. He was very pale, and had a restless light in his eye that I did not remember to have observed before. The anxious lines, too, about his mouth were deepened, and there was a cavernous, hollow look about his cheeks and temples which seemed to speak of sickness or sorrow. He had glanced at me as he came in, but without any gleam of recognition in his face. Now he glanced again, as I fancied, somewhat doubtfully. When he did so for the third or fourth time I ventured to address him.

"Mr. John Dwerrihouse, I think?"

"That is my name," he replied.

"I had the pleasure of meeting you at Dumbleton about three years ago."

Mr. Dwerrihouse bowed.

"I thought I knew your face," he said; "but your name, I regret to say—"

"Langford—William Langford. I have known Jonathan Jelf since we were boys together at Merchant Taylor's, and I generally spend a few weeks at Dumbleton in the shooting season. I suppose we are bound for the same destination?"

"Not if you are on your way to the manor," he replied. "I am travelling upon business—rather troublesome business too—while you, doubtless, have only pleasure in view."

"Just so. I am in the habit of looking forward to this visit as to the brightest three weeks in all the year."

"It is a pleasant house," said Mr. Dwerrihouse.

"The pleasantest I know."

"And Jelf is thoroughly hospitable."

"The best and kindest fellow in the world!"

"They have invited me to spend Christmas week with them," pursued Mr. Dwerrihouse, after a moment's pause.

"And you are coming?"

"I cannot tell. It must depend on the issue of this business which I have in hand. You have heard perhaps that we are about to construct a branch line from Blackwater to Stockbridge." I explained that I had been for some months away from England, and had therefore heard nothing of the contemplated improvement. Mr. Dwerrihouse smiled complacently.

"It *will* be an improvement," he said, "a great improvement. Stockbridge is a flourishing town, and needs but a more direct railway communication with the metropolis to become an important centre of commerce. This branch was my own idea. I brought the project before the board, and have myself superintended the execution of it up to the present time."

"You are an East Anglian director, I presume?"

"My interest in the company," replied Mr. Dwerrihouse, "is threefold. I am a director, I am a considerable shareholder, and, as head of the firm of Dwerrihouse, Dwerrihouse & Craik, I am the company's principal solicitor."

Loquacious, self-important, full of his pet project, and apparently unable to talk on any other subject, Mr. Dwerrihouse then went on to tell of the opposition he had encountered and the obstacles he had overcome in the cause of the Stockbridge branch. I was entertained with a multitude of local details and local grievances. The rapacity of one squire, the impracticability of another, the indignation of the rector whose glebe was threatened, the culpable indifference of the Stockbridge townspeople, who could not *be* brought to see that their most vital interests hinged upon a junction with the Great East Anglian line; the spite of the local newspaper, and the unheard-of difficulties attending the Common question, were each and all laid before me with a circumstantiality that possessed the deepest interest for my excellent fellow-traveller, but none whatever for myself. From these, to my despair, he went on to more intricate matters: to the approximate expenses of construction per mile; to the estimates sent in by different contractors; to the probable traffic returns of the new line; to the provisional clauses of the new act as enumerated in Schedule D of the company's last half-yearly report; and so on and on and on, till my head ached and my attention flagged and my eyes kept closing in spite of every effort that I made to keep them open. At length I was roused by these words:

"Seventy-five thousand pounds, cash down."

"Seventy-five thousand pounds, cash down," I repeated, in the liveliest tone I could assume. "That is a heavy sum."

"A heavy sum to carry here," replied Mr. Dwerrihouse, pointing significantly to his breastpocket, "but a mere fraction of what we shall ultimately have to pay."

"You do not mean to say that you have seventy-five thousand pounds at this moment upon your person?" I exclaimed.

"My good sir, have I not been telling you so for the last

half-hour?" said Mr. Dwerrihouse, testily. "That money has to be paid over at half-past eight o'clock this evening, at the office of Sir Thomas's solicitors, on completion of the deed of sale."

"But how will you get across by night from Blackwater to Stockbridge with seventy-five thousand pounds in your pocket?"

"To Stockbridge!" echoed the lawyer. "I find I have made myself very imperfectly understood. I thought I had explained how this sum only carries us as far as Mallingford,—the first stage, as it were, of our journey,—and how our route from Blackwater to Mallingford lies entirely through Sir Thomas Liddell's property."

"I beg your pardon," I stammered. "I fear my thoughts were wandering. So you only go as far as Mallingford tonight?"

"Precisely. I shall get a conveyance from the 'Blackwater Arms.' And you?"

"Oh, Jelf sends a trap to meet me at Clayborough! Can I be the bearer of any message from you?"

"You may say, if you please, Mr. Langford, that I wished I could have been your companion all the way, and that I will come over, if possible, before Christmas."

"Nothing more?"

Mr. Dwerrihouse smiled grimly. "Well," he said, "you may tell my cousin that she need not burn the hall down in my honour this time, and that I shall be obliged if she will order the blue-room chimney to be swept before I arrive."

"That sounds tragic. Had you a conflagration on the occasion of your last visit to Dumbleton?"

"Something like it. There had been no fire lighted in my bedroom since the spring, the flue was foul, and the rooks had built in it; so when I went up to dress for dinner I found the room full of smoke and the chimney on fire. Are we already at Blackwater?"

The train had gradually come to a pause while Mr. Dwerrihouse was speaking, and, on putting my head out of the window, I could see the station some few hundred yards ahead. There was another train before us blocking the way, and the guard was making use of the delay to collect the Blackwater tickets. I had scarcely ascertained our position when the ruddy-faced official appeared at our carriage door.

"Tickets, sir!" said he.

"I am for Clayborough," I replied, holding out the tiny pink card.

He took it, glanced at it by the light of his little lantern, gave it back, looked, as I fancied, somewhat sharply at my fellow-traveller, and disappeared.

"He did not ask for yours," I said, with some surprise.

"They never do," replied Mr. Dwerrihouse; "they all know me, and of course I travel free."

"Blackwater! Blackwater!" cried the porter, running along the platform beside us as we glided into the station.

Mr. Dwerrihouse pulled out his deed-box, put his travelling-cap in his pocket, resumed his hat, took down his umbrella, and prepared to be gone.

"Many thanks, Mr. Langford, for your society," he said, with old-fashioned courtesy. "I wish you a good-evening."

"Good-evening," I replied, putting out my hand.

But he either did not see it or did not choose to see it, and, slightly lifting his hat, stepped out upon the platform. Having done this, he moved slowly away and mingled with the departing crowd.

Leaning forward to watch him out of sight, I trod upon something which proved to be a cigar-case. It had fallen, no doubt, from the pocket of his waterproof coat, and was made of dark morocco leather, with a silver monogram upon the side. I sprang out of the carriage just as the guard came up to lock me in.

Is there one minute to spare?" I asked, eagerly. "The gentleman who travelled down with me from town has dropped his cigar-case—he is not yet out of the station!"

"Just a minute and a half, sir," replied the guard. "You must be quick."

"I dashed along the platform as fast as my feet could carry me. It was a large station, and Mr. Dwerrihouse had by this time got more than half-way to the farther end.

I, however, saw him distinctly, moving slowly with the

stream. Then, as I drew nearer, I saw that he had met some friend,—that they were talking as they walked,—that they presently fell back somewhat from the crowd and stood aside in earnest conversation. I made straight for the spot where they were waiting. There was a vivid gas-jet just above their heads, and the light fell full upon their faces. I saw both distinctly—the face of Mr. Dwerrihouse and the face of his companion. Running, breathless, eager as I was, getting in the way of porters and passengers, and fearful every instant lest I should see the train going on without me, I yet observed that the new-comer was considerably younger and shorter than the director, that he was sandy-haired, mustachioed, small-featured, and dressed in a close-cut suit of Scotch tweed. I was now within a few yards of them. I ran against a stout gentleman, I was nearly knocked down by a luggage-truck, I stumbled over a carpet-bag, I gained the spot just as the driver's whistle warned me to return.

To my utter stupefaction, they were no longer there. I had seen them but two seconds before—and they were gone! I stood still. I looked to right and left. I saw no sign of them in any direction. It was as if the platform had gaped and swallowed them.

"There were two gentlemen standing here a moment ago," I said to a porter at my elbow; "which way can they have gone?"

"I saw no gentlemen, sir," replied the man. The whistle shrilled out again. The guard, far up the platform, held up his arm, and shouted to me to "come on!"

"If you're going on by this train, sir," said the porter, "you must run for it."

I did run for it, just gained the carriage as the train began to move, was shoved in by the guard, and left, breathless and bewildered, with Mr. Dwerrihouse's cigar-case still in my hand.

It was the strangest disappearance in the world; it was like a transformation trick in a pantomime. They were there one moment—palpably there, walking, with the gaslight full upon their faces—and the next moment they were gone. There was no door near, no window, no staircase; it was a mere slip of barren platform, tapestried with big advertisements. Could anything be more mysterious?

It was not worth thinking about; and yet, for my life, I could not help pondering upon it—pondering, wondering, conjecturing, turning it over and over in my mind, and beating my brains for a solution of the enigma. I thought of it all the way from Blackwater to Clayborough. I thought of it all the way from Clayborough to Dumbleton, as I rattled along the smooth highway in a trim dog-cart, drawn by a splendid black mare and driven by the silentest and dapperest of East Anglian grooms.

We did the nine miles in something less than an hour, and pulled up before the lodge-gates just as the church clock was striking half-past seven. A couple of minutes more, and the warm glow of the lighted hall was flooding out upon the gravel, a hearty grasp was on my hand, and a clear jovial voice was bidding me "welcome to Dumbleton."

"And now, my dear fellow," said my host, when the first greeting was over, "you have no time to spare. We dine at eight, and there are people coming to meet you, so you must just get the dressing business over as quickly as may be. By the way, you will meet some acquaintances; the Biddulphs are coming, and Prendergast (Prendergast of the Skirmishers) is staying in the house. Adieu! Mrs. Jelf will be expecting you in the drawing-room."

I was ushered to my room—not the blue room, of which Mr. Dwerrihouse had made disagreeable experience, but a pretty little bachelor's chamber, hung with a delicate chintz and made cheerful by a blazing fire. I unlocked my portmanteau. I tried to be expeditious; but the memory of my railway adventure haunted me. I could not get free of it. I could not shake it off. It impeded me, it worried me, it tripped me up, it caused me to mislay my studs, to mistie my cravat, to wrench the buttons off my gloves. Worst of all, it made me so late that the party had all assembled before I reached the drawing-room. I had scarcely paid my respects to Mrs. Jelf when dinner was announced, and we paired off, some eight or ten couples strong, into the dining-room.

I am not going to describe either the guests or the dinner.

All provincial parties bear the strictest family resemblance, and I am not aware that an East Anglian banquet offers any exception to the rule. There was the usual country baronet and his wife; there were the usual country parsons and their wives; there was the sempiternal turkey and haunch of venison. *Vanitas vanitatum.* There is nothing new under the sun.

I was placed about midway down the table. I had taken one rector's wife down to dinner, and I had another at my left hand. They talked across me, and their talk was about babies; it was dreadfully dull. At length there came a pause. The entrees had just been removed, and the turkey had come upon the scene. The conversation had all along been of the languidest, but at this moment it happened to have stagnated altogether. Jelf was carving the turkey; Mrs. Jelf looked as if she was trying to think of something to say; everybody else was silent. Moved by an unlucky impulse, I thought I would relate my adventure.

"By the way, Jelf," I began, "I came down part of the way to-day with a friend of yours."

"Indeed!" said the master of the feast, slicing scientifically into the breast of the turkey. "With whom, pray?"

"With one who bade me tell you that he should, if possible, pay you a visit before Christmas."

"I cannot think who that could be," said my friend, smiling.

"It must be Major Thorp," suggested Mrs. Jelf.

I shook my head.

"It was not Major Thorp," I replied, "it was a near relation of your own, Mrs. Jelf."

"Then I am more puzzled than ever," replied my hostess. "Pray tell me who it was."

"It was no less a person than your cousin, Mr. John Dwerrihouse."

Jonathan Jelf laid down his knife and fork. Mrs. Jelf looked at me in a strange, startled way, and said never a word.

"And he desired me to tell you, my dear madam, that you need not take the trouble to burn the hall down in his honour this time, but only to have the chimney of the blue room swept before his arrival."

Before I had reached the end of my sentence I became aware of something ominous in the faces of the guests. I felt I had said something which I had better have left unsaid, and that for some unexplained reason my words had evoked a general consternation. I sat confounded, not daring to utter another syllable, and for at least two whole minutes there was dead silence round the table. Then Captain Prendergast came to the rescue.

"You have been abroad for some months, have you not, Mr. Langford?" he said, with the desperation of one who flings himself into the breach.

"I heard you had been to Russia. Surely you have something to tell us of the state and temper of the country after the war?"

I was heartily grateful to the gallant Skirmisher for this diversion in my favour. I answered him, I fear, somewhat lamely; but he kept the conversation up, and presently one or two others joined in and so the difficulty, whatever it might have been, was bridged over—bridged over, but not repaired. A something, an awkwardness, a visible constraint remained. The guests hitherto had been simply dull, but now they were evidently uncomfortable and embarrassed.

The dessert had scarcely been placed upon the table when the ladies left the room. I seized the opportunity to select a vacant chair next Captain Prendergast.

"In heaven's name," I whispered, "what was the matter just now? What had I said?"

"You mentioned the name of John Dwerrihouse."

"What of that? I had seen him not two hours before."

"It is a most astounding circumstance that you should have seen him," said Captain Prendergast. "Are you sure it was he?"

"As sure as of my own identity. We were talking all the way between London and Blackwater. But why does that surprise you?"

"*Because,*" replied Captain Prendergast, dropping his voice to the lowest whisper—"*because John Dwerrihouse absconded three months ago with seventy-five thousand pounds of the company's money, and has never been heard of since.*"

John Dwerrihouse had absconded three months ago—and I had seen him only a few hours back! John Dwerrihouse had embezzled seventy-five thousand pounds of the company's money, yet told me that he carried that sum upon his person! Were ever facts so strangely incongruous, so difficult to reconcile? How should he have ventured again into the light of day? How dared he show himself along the line? Above all, what had he been doing throughout those mysterious three months of disappearance?

Perplexing questions these—questions which at once suggested themselves to the minds of all concerned, but which admitted of no easy solution. I could find no reply to them. Captain Prendergast had not even a suggestion to offer. Jonathan Jelf, who seized the first opportunity of drawing me aside and learning all that I had to tell, was more amazed and bewildered than either of us. He came to my room that night, when all the guests were gone, and we talked the thing over from every point of view; without, it must be confessed, arriving at any kind of conclusion.

"I do not ask you," he said," whether you can have mistaken your man. That is impossible."

"As impossible as that I should mistake some stranger for yourself."

"It is not a question of looks or voice, but of facts. That he should have alluded to the fire in the blue room is proof enough of John Dwerrihouse's identity. How did he look?"

"Older, I thought; considerably older, paler, and more anxious."

He has had enough to make him look anxious, anyhow, "said my friend, gloomily, "be he innocent or guilty."

"I am inclined to believe that he is innocent," I replied. "He showed no embarrassment when I addressed him, and no uneasiness when the guard came round. His conversation was open to a fault. I might almost say that he talked too freely of the business which he had in hand."

"That again is strange, for I know no one more reticent on such subjects. He actually told you that he had the seventy-five thousand pounds in his pocket?"

"He did."

"Humph! My wife has an idea about it, and she may be right—"

"What idea?"

"Well, she fancies,—women are so clever, you know, at putting themselves inside people's motives—she fancies that he was tempted, that he did actually take the money, and that he has been concealing himself these three months in some wild part of the country, struggling possibly with his conscience all the time, and daring neither to abscond with his booty nor to come back and restore it."

"But now that he has come back?"

"That is the point. She conceives that he has probably thrown himself upon the company's mercy, made restitution of the money, and, being forgiven, is permitted to carry the business through as if nothing whatever had happened."

"The last," I replied, "is an impossible case. Mrs. Jelf thinks like a generous and delicate minded woman, but not in the least like a board of railway directors. They would never carry forgiveness so far."

"I fear not; and yet it is the only conjecture that bears a semblance of likelihood. However we can run over to Clayborough tomorrow and see if anything is to be learned. By the way Prendergast tells me you picked up his cigar-case."

"I did so, and here it is."

Jelf took the cigar-case, examined it by the light of the lamp, and said at once that it was beyond doubt Mr. Dwerrihouse's property, and that he remembered to have seen him use it.

"Here, too, is his monogram on the side," he added—"a big J transfixing a capital D. He used to carry the same on his note-paper."

"It offers, at all events, a proof that I was not dreaming."

"Ay, but it is time you were asleep and dreaming now. I am ashamed to have kept you up so long. Good night."

"Good-night, and remember that I am more than ready to go with you to Clayborough or Blackwater or London or anywhere, if I can be of the least service."

"Thanks! I know you mean it, old friend, and it may be that I shall put you to the test. Once more, good-night."

So we parted for that night, and met again in the breakfast-room at half-past eight next morning. It was a hurried, silent, uncomfortable meal; none of us had slept well, and all were thinking of the same subject. Mrs. Jelf had evidently been crying. Jelf was impatient to be off, and both Captain Prendergast and myself felt ourselves to be in the painful position of outsiders who are involuntarily brought into a domestic trouble. Within twenty minutes after we had left the breakfast-table the dog-cart was brought round, and my friend and I were on the road to Clayborough.

"Tell you what it is, Langford," he said, as we sped along between the wintry hedges," I do not much fancy to bring up Dwerrihouse's name at Clayborough. All the officials know that he is my wife's relation, and the subject just now is hardly a pleasant one. If you don't much mind, we will make the 11:10 to Blackwater. It's an important station, and we shall stand a far better chance of picking up information there than at Clayborough."

So we took the 11:10, which happened to be an express, and, arriving at Blackwater about a quarter before twelve, proceeded at once to prosecute our inquiry.

We began by asking for the station-master, a big, blunt, businesslike person, who at once averred that he knew Mr. John Dwerrihouse perfectly well, and that there was no director on the line whom he had seen and spoken to so frequently.

"He used to be down here two or three times a week about three months ago," said he, "when the new line was first set afoot; but since then, you know, gentlemen—"

He paused significantly.

Jelf flushed scarlet.

"Yes, yes," he said, hurriedly; "we know all about that. The point now to be ascertained is whether anything has been seen or heard of him lately."

"Not to my knowledge," replied the stationmaster.

"He is not known to have been down the line any time yesterday, for instance?"

The station-master shook his head.

"The East Anglian, sir," said he, "is about the last place where he would dare to show himself. Why, there isn't a station-master, there isn't guard, there isn't a porter, who doesn't know Mr. Dwerrihouse by sight as well as he knows his own face in the looking-glass, or who wouldn't telegraph for the police as soon as he had set eyes on him at any point along the line. Bless you, sir! there's been a standing order out against him ever since the 25th of September last."

"And yet," pursued my friend, "a gentleman who travelled down yesterday from London to Clayborough by the afternoon express testifies that he saw Mr. Dwerrihouse in the train, and that Mr. Dwerrihouse alighted at Blackwater station."

"Quite impossible, sir," replied the station-master promptly.

"Why impossible?"

"Because there is no station along the line where he is so well known or where he would run so great a risk. It would be just running his head into the lion's mouth; he would have been mad to come nigh Blackwater station; and if he had come he would have been arrested before he left the platform."

"Can you tell me who took the Blackwater tickets of that train?"

"I can, sir. It was the guard, Benjamin Somers."

"And where can I find him?"

"You can find him, sir, by staying here, if you please, till one o'clock. He will be coming through with the up express from Crampton, which stays in Blackwater for ten minutes."

We waited for the up express, beguiling the time as best we could by strolling along the Blackwater road till we came almost to the outskirts of the town, from which the station was distant nearly a couple of miles. By one o'clock we were back again upon the platform and waiting for the train. It came punctually, and I at once recognised the ruddy-faced guard who had gone down with my train the evening before.

"The gentlemen want to ask you something about Mr. Dwerrihouse, Somers," said the station-master, by way of introduction. The guard flashed a keen glance from my face to Jelf's and back again to mine.

"Mr. John Dwerrihouse, the late director?" said he, interrogatively.

"The same," replied my friend. "Should you know him if you saw him?"

"Anywhere, sir."

"Do you know if he was in the 4:15 express yesterday afternoon?"

"He was not, sir."

"How can you answer so positively?"

"Because I looked into every carriage and saw every face in that train, and I could take my oath that Mr. Dwerrihouse was not in it. This gentleman was," he added, turning sharply upon me. "I don't know that I ever saw him before in my life, but I remember his face perfectly. You nearly missed taking your seat in time at this station, sir, and you got out at Clayborough."

"Quite true, guard," I replied; "but do you not remember the face of the gentleman who travelled down in the same carriage with me as far as here?"

"It was my impression, sir, that you travelled down alone," said Somers, with a look of some surprise.

"By no means. I had a fellow-traveller as far as Blackwater, and it was in trying to restore him the cigar-case which he had dropped in the carriage that I so nearly let you go on without me."

"I remember your saying something about a cigar-case, certainly," replied the guard; "but—"

"You asked for my ticket just before we entered station."

"I did, sir."

"Then you must have seen him. He sat in the corner next the very door to which you came."

"No, indeed; I saw no one."

I looked at Jelf. I began to think the guard was in the ex-director's confidence, and paid for his silence.

"If I had seen another traveller I should have asked for his ticket," added Somers. "Did you see me ask for his ticket, sir?"

"I observed that you did not ask for it, but he explained that by saying—" I hesitated. I feared I might be telling too much, and so broke off abruptly.

The guard and the station-master exchanged glances. The former looked impatiently at his watch.

"I am obliged to go on in four minutes more sir," he said.

"One last question, then," interposed Jelf, with a sort of

desperation. "If this gentleman's fellow traveller had been Mr. John Dwerrihouse, and he had been sitting in the corner next the door in which you took the tickets, could you have failed to see and recognise him?"

"No, sir; it would have been quite impossible!"

"And you are certain you did not see him?"

"As I said before, sir, I could take my oath, I did not see him. And if it wasn't that I don't like to contradict a gentleman, I would say I could also take my oath that this gentlemen was quite alone in the carriage the whole way from London to Clayborough. Why, sir," he added dropping his voice so as to be inaudible to the station-master, who had been called away to speak to some person close by, "you expressly asked me to give you a compartment to yourself, and I did so. I locked you in, and you were so good as to give me something for myself."

"Yes; but Mr. Dwerrihouse had a key of his own."

"I never saw him, sir; I saw no one in that compartment but yourself. Beg pardon, sir; my time's up." And with this the ruddy guard touched his cap and was gone. In another minute the heavy panting of the engine began afresh, and the "train" glided slowly out of the station.

We looked at each other for some moments in silence. I was the first to speak.

"Mr. Benjamin Somers knows more than he chooses to tell," I said.

"Humph! do you think so?"

"It must be. He could not have come to the door without seeing him; it's impossible."

"There is one thing not impossible, my dear fellow."

"What is that?"

"That you may have fallen asleep and dreamed the whole thing."

"Could I dream of a branch line that I had never heard of? Could I dream of a hundred and one business details that had no kind of interest for me? Could I dream of the seventy-five thousand pounds?"

"Perhaps you might have seen or heard some vague account of the affair while you were abroad. It might have made no impression upon you at the time, and might have come back to you in your dreams, recalled perhaps by the mere names of the stations on the line."

"What about the fire in the chimney of the blue room—should I have heard of that during my journey?"

"Well, no; I admit there is a difficulty about that point."

"And what about the cigar-case?"

"Ay, by Jove! there is the cigar-case. That is a stubborn fact. Well, it's a mysterious affair, and it will need a better detective than myself, I fancy, to clear it up. I suppose we may as well go home."

A week had not gone by when I received a letter from the secretary of the East Anglian Railway Company, requesting the favour of my attendance at a special board meeting not then many days distant. No reasons were alleged and no apologies offered for this demand upon my time, but they had heard, it was clear, of my inquiries anent the missing director, and had a mind to put me through some sort of official examination upon the subject. Being still a guest at Dumbleton Hall, I had to go up to London for the purpose and Jonathan Jelf accompanied me. I found the direction of the Great East Anglian line represented by a party of some twelve or fourteen gentlemen seated in solemn conclave round a huge green baize table, in a gloomy board room adjoining the London terminus.

Being courteously received by the chairman (who at once began by saying that certain statements of mine respecting Mr. John Dwerrihouse had come to the knowledge of the direction, and that they in consequence desired to confer with me on those points), we were placed at the table and the inquiry proceeded in due form.

I was first asked if I knew Mr. John Dwerrihouse, how long I had been acquainted with him, and whether I could identify him at sight. I was then asked when I had seen him last. To which I replied, "On the 4th of this present month, December, 1856." Then came the inquiry of where I had seen him on that fourth day of December; to which I replied that I met him in a first-class compartment of the 4:15 down express, that he got in just as the train was leaving the London terminus, and that he alighted at Blackwater station. The chairman then inquired whether I had held any communication with my fellow-traveller; whereupon I related, as nearly as I could remember it, the whole bulk and substance of Mr. John Dwerrihouse's diffuse information respecting the new branch line.

To all this the board listened with profound attention, while the chairman presided and the secretary took notes. I then produced the cigar-case. It was passed from hand to hand, and recognized by all. There was not a man present who did not remember that plain cigar-case with its silver monogram, or to whom it seemed anything less entirely corroborative of my evidence. When at length I had told all that I had to tell, the chairman whispered something to the secretary; the secretary touched a silver hand-bell, and the guard, Benjamin Somers, was ushered into the room. He was then examined as carefully as myself. He declared that he knew Mr. John Dwerrihouse perfectly well, that he could not be mistaken in him, that he remembered going down with the 4:15 express on the afternoon in question, that he remembered me, and that, there being one or two empty first-class compartments on that especial afternoon, he had, in compliance with my request, placed me in a carriage by myself. He was positive that I remained alone in that compartment all the way from London to Clayborough. He was ready to take his oath that Dwerrihouse was neither in that carriage with me nor in any compartment of that train. He remembered distinctly to have examined my ticket to Blackwater; was certain that there was no one else at that time in the carriage; could not have failed to observe a second person, if there had been one; had that second person been Mr. John Dwerrihouse, should have quietly double-locked the door of the carriage and have at once given information to the Blackwater station-master. So clear, so decisive, so ready, was Somers with this testimony, that the board looked fairly puzzled.

"You hear this person's statement, Mr. Langford," said the chairman. "It contradicts yours in every particular. What have you to say in reply?"

"I can only repeat what I said before. I am quite as positive of the truth of my own assertions as Mr. Somers can be of the truth of his."

"You say that Mr. Dwerrihouse alighted in Blackwater, and that he was in possession of a private key. Are you sure that he had not alighted by means of that key before the guard came round for the tickets?"

"I am quite positive that he did not leave the carriage till the train had fairly entered the station, and the other Blackwater passengers alighted. I even saw that he was met there by a friend."

"Indeed! Did you see that person distinctly?"

"Quite distinctly."

"Can you describe his appearance?"

"I think so. He was short and very slight, sandy-haired, with a bushy moustache and beard, and he wore a closely fitting suit of gray tweed. His age I should take to be about thirty-eight or forty."

"Did Mr. Dwerrihouse leave the station in this person's company?"

"I cannot tell. I saw them walking together down the platform, and then I saw them standing inside under a gas-jet, talking earnestly. After that I lost sight of them quite suddenly, and just then my train went on, and I with it."

The chairman and secretary conferred together in an undertone. The directors whispered to one another. One or two looked suspiciously at the guard. I could see that my evidence remained unshaken, and that, like myself, they suspected some complicity between the guard and the defaulter.

"How far did you conduct that 4:15 express on the day in question, Somers?" asked the chairman. "All through, sir," replied the guard, "from London to Crampton."

"How was it that you were not relieved at Clayborough? I thought there was always a change of guards at Clayborough."

"There used to be, sir, till the new regulations came in force last midsummer, since when the guards in charge of express trains go the whole way through."

The chairman turned to the secretary.

"I think it would be as well," he said, "if we had the daybook to refer to upon this point."

Again the secretary touched the silver handbell, and desired the porter in attendance to summon Mr. Raikes. From a word or two dropped by another of the directors I gathered that Mr. Raikes was one of the under-secretaries.

He came,—a small, slight, sandy-haired, keen-eyed man, with an eager, nervous manner, and a forest of light beard and moustache. He just showed himself at the door of the board room, and, being requested to bring a certain day-book from a certain shelf in a certain room, bowed and vanished.

He was there such a moment, and the surprise of seeing him was so great and sudden, that it was not till the door had closed upon him that I found voice to speak. He was no sooner gone, however, than I sprang to my feet.

"That person," I said, "is the same who met Mr. Dwerrihouse upon the platform at Blackwater!"

There was a general movement of surprise. The chairman looked grave and somewhat agitated.

"Take care, Mr. Langford," he said; "take care what you say."

"I am as positive of his identity as of my own."

"Do you consider the consequences of your words? Do you consider that you are bringing a charge of the gravest character against one of the company's servants?"

"I am willing to be put upon my oath, if necessary. The man who came to that door a minute since is the same whom I saw talking with Mr. Dwerrihouse on the Blackwater platform. Were he twenty times the company's servant, I could say neither more nor less."

The chairman turned again to the guard.

"Did you see Mr. Raikes in the train or on the platform?" he asked.

Somers shook his head.

"I am confident Mr. Raikes was not in the train," he said, "and I certainly did not see him on the platform."

The chairman turned next to the secretary.

"Mr. Raikes is in your office, Mr. Hunter," he said. "Can you remember if he was absent on the 4th instant?"

"I do not think he was," replied the secretary, "but I am not prepared to speak positively. I have been away most afternoons myself lately, and Mr. Raikes might easily have absented himself if he had been disposed."

At this moment the under-secretary returned with the day-book under his arm.

"Be pleased to refer, Mr. Raikes," said the chairman, "to the entries of the 4th instant, and see what Benjamin Somers's duties were on that day."

Mr. Raikes threw open the cumbrous volume, and ran a practised eye and finger down some three or four successive columns of entries. Stopping suddenly at the foot of a page, he then read aloud that Benjamin Somers had on that day conducted the 4:15 express from London to Crampton.

The chairman leaned forward in his seat, looked the under-secretary full in the face, and said, quite sharply and suddenly:

"Where were *you*, Mr. Raikes, on the same afternoon?"

"*I*, sir?"

"You, Mr. Raikes. Where were you on the afternoon and evening of the 4th of the present month?"

"Here, sir, in Mr. Hunter's office. Where else should I be?"

There was a dash of trepidation in the under-secretary's voice as he said this, but his look of surprise was natural enough.

"We have some reason for believing, Mr. Raikes, that you were absent that afternoon without leave. Was this the case?"

"Certainly not, sir. I have not had a day's holiday since September. Mr. Hunter will bear me out in this." Mr. Hunter repeated what he had previously said on the subject, but added that the clerks in the adjoining office would be certain to know. Whereupon the senior clerk, a grave, middle-aged person in green glasses, was summoned and interrogated.

His testimony cleared the under-secretary at once. He declared that Mr. Raikes had in no instance, to his knowledge, been absent during office hours since his return from his annual holiday in September.

I was confounded. The chairman turned to me with a smile, in which a shade of covert annoyance was scarcely apparent.

"You hear, Mr. Langford?" he said.

"I hear, sir; but my conviction remains unshaken."

"I fear, Mr. Langford, that your convictions are very insufficiently based," replied the chairman, with a doubtful cough." I fear that you 'dream dreams,' and mistake them for actual occurrences. It is a dangerous habit of mind, and might lead to dangerous results. Mr. Raikes here would have found himself in an unpleasant position had he not proved so satisfactory an alibi."

I was about to reply, but he gave me no time.

"I think, gentlemen," he went on to say, addressing the board," that we should be wasting time to push this inquiry further. Mr. Langford's evidence would seem to be of an equal value throughout. The testimony of Benjamin Somers disproves his first statement, and the testimony of the last witness disproves his second. I think we may conclude that Mr. Langford fell asleep in the train on the occasion of his journey to Clayborough, and dreamed an unusually vivid and circumstantial dream, of which, however, we have now heard quite enough."

There are few things more annoying than to find one's positive convictions met with incredulity. I could not help feeling impatience at the turn that affairs had taken. I was not proof against the civil sarcasm of the chairman's manner. Most intolerable of all, however, was the quiet smile lurking about the corners of Benjamin Somers's mouth, and the half-triumphant, half-malicious gleam in the eyes of the under-secretary. The man was evidently puzzled and somewhat alarmed. His looks seemed furtively to interrogate me. Who was I? What did I want? Why had I come there to do him an ill turn with his employers? What was it to me whether or no he was absent without leave?

Seeing all this, and perhaps more irritated by it than the thing deserved, I begged leave to detain the attention of the board for a moment longer. Jelf plucked me impatiently by the sleeve.

"Better let the thing drop," he whispered. "The chairman's right enough; you dreamed it, and the less said now the better."

I was not to be silenced, however, in this fashion. I had yet something to say, and I would say it. It was to this effect: that dreams were not usually productive of tangible results, and that I requested to know in what way the chairman conceived I had evolved from my dream so substantial and well-made a delusion as the cigar-case which I had had the honour to place before him at the commencement of our interview.

"The cigar-case, I admit, Mr. Langford," the chairman replied, "is a very strong point in your evidence. It is your only strong point, however, and there is just a possibility that we may all be misled by a mere accidental resemblance. Will you permit me to see the case again?"

"It is unlikely," I said, as I handed it to him, "that any other should bear precisely this monogram, and yet be in all other particulars exactly similar."

The chairman examined it for a moment in silence, and then passed it to Mr. Hunter. Mr. Hunter turned it over and over, and shook his head.

"This is no mere resemblance," he said. "It is John Dwerrihouse's cigar-case to a certainty. I remember it perfectly; I have seen it a hundred times."

"I believe I may say the same," added the chairman; "yet how account for the way in which Mr. Langford asserts that it came into his possession?"

"I can only repeat," I replied, "that I found it on the floor of the carriage after Mr. Dwerrihouse had alighted. It was in leaning out to look after him that I trod upon it, and it was in running after him for the purpose of restoring it that I saw or believed I saw, Mr. Raikes standing aside with him in earnest conversation."

Again I felt Jonathan Jelf plucking at my sleeve.

"Look at Raikes," he whispered; "look at Raikes!"

I turned to where the under-secretary had been standing a moment before, and saw him, white as death, with lips trembling and livid, stealing toward the door.

To conceive a sudden, strange, and indefinite suspicion, to fling myself in his way, to take him by the shoulders as if he were a child, and turn his craven face, perforce, toward the board, were with me the work of an instant.

"Look at him!" I exclaimed. "Look at his face! I ask no better witness to the truth of my words."

The chairman's brow darkened.

"Mr. Raikes," he said, sternly, "if you know anything you had better speak."

Vainly trying to wrench himself from my grasp, the under-secretary stammered out an incoherent denial.

"Let me go," he said. "I know nothing—you have no right to detain me—let me go!"

"Did you, or did you not, meet Mr. John Dwerrihouse at Blackwater station? The charge brought against you is either true or false. If true, you will do well to throw yourself upon the mercy of the board and make full confession of all that you know."

The under-secretary wrung his hands in an agony of helpless terror.

"I was away!" he cried. "I was two hundred miles away at the time! I know nothing about it—I have nothing to confess—I am innocent—I call God to witness I am innocent!"

"Two hundred miles away!" echoed the chairman. "What do you mean?"

"I was in Devonshire. I had three weeks' leave of absence—I appeal to Mr. Hunter—Mr. Hunter knows I had three weeks' leave of absence! I was in Devonshire all the time; I can prove I was in Devonshire!"

Seeing him so abject, so incoherent, so wild with apprehension, the directors began to whisper gravely among themselves, while one got quietly up and called the porter to guard the door.

"What has your being in Devonshire to do with the matter?" said the chairman. "When were you in Devonshire?"

"Mr. Raikes took his leave in September," said the secretary, "about the time when Mr. Dwerrihouse disappeared."

"I never even heard that he had disappeared till I came back!"

"That must remain to be proved," said the chairman. "I shall at once put this matter in the hands of the police. In the meanwhile, Mr. Raikes, being myself a magistrate and used to deal with these cases, I advise you to offer no resistance but to confess while confession may yet do you service. As for your accomplice—"

The frightened wretch fell upon his knees.

"I had no accomplice!" he cried, "Only have mercy upon me—only spare my life, and I will confess all! I didn't mean to harm him! I didn't mean to hurt a hair of his head! Only have mercy upon me, and let me go!"

The chairman rose in his place, pale and agitated.

"Good heavens!" he exclaimed, "what horrible mystery is this? What does it mean?"

"As sure as there is a God in heaven," said Jonathan Jelf, "it means that murder has been done."

"No! no! no!" shrieked Raikes, still upon his knees, and cowering like a beaten hound, "Not murder! No jury that ever sat could bring it in murder. I thought I had only stunned him—I never meant to do more than stun him! Manslaughter—manslaughter—not murder!"

Overcome by the horror of this unexpected revelation, the chairman covered his face with his hand and for a moment or two remained silent.

"Miserable man," he said at length, "you have betrayed yourself."

"You bade me confess! You urged me to throw myself upon the mercy of the board!"

"You have confessed to a crime which no one suspected you of having committed," replied the chairman, "and which this board has no power either to punish or forgive. All that I can do for you is to advise you to submit to the law, to plead guilty, and to conceal nothing. When did you do this deed?"

The guilty man rose to his feet, and leaned heavily against the table. His answer came reluctantly, like the speech of one dreaming.

"On the 22d of September!"

On the 22d of September! I looked in Jonathan Jelf's face, and he in mine. I felt my own smiling with a strange sense of wonder and dread. I saw his blanch suddenly, even to the lips.

"Merciful Heaven!" he whispered. *"What was it, then, that you saw in the train?"*

What was it that I saw in the train? That question remains unanswered to this day. I have never been able to reply to it. I only know that it bore the living likeness of the murdered man, whose body had then been lying some ten weeks under a rough pile of branches and brambles and rotting leaves, at the bottom of a deserted chalk-pit about half-way between Blackwater and Mallingford. I know that it spoke and moved and looked as that man spoke and moved and looked in life; that I heard, or seemed to hear, things revealed which I could never otherwise have learned; that I was guided, as it were, by that vision on the platform to the identification of the murderer; and that, a passive instrument myself, I was destined, by means of these mysterious teachings to bring about the ends of justice. For these things I have never been able to account.

As for that matter of the cigar-case, it proved, on inquiry, that the carriage in which I travelled down that afternoon to Clayborough had not been in use for several weeks, and was, in point of fact, the same in which poor John Dwerrihouse had performed his last journey. The case had doubtless been dropped by him, and had lain unnoticed till I found it.

Upon the details of the murder I have no need to dwell. Those who desire more ample particulars may find them, and the written confession of Augustus Raikes, in the files of the "Times" for 1856. Enough that the under-secretary, knowing the history of the new line, and following the negotiation step by step through all its stages, determined to waylay Mr. Dwerrihouse, rob him of the seventy-five thousand pounds, and escape to America with his booty.

In order to effect these ends he obtained leave of absence a few days before the time appointed for the payment of the money, secured his passage across the Atlantic in a steamer advertised to start on the 23d, provided himself with a heavily loaded "life-preserver," and went down to Blackwater to await the arrival of his victim. How he met him on the platform with a pretended message from the board, how he offered to conduct him by a short cut across the fields to Mallingford, how, having brought him to a lonely place, he struck him down with the life-preserver, and so killed him, and how, finding what he had done, he dragged the body to the verge of an out-of-the-way chalk-pit, and there flung it in and piled it over with branches and brambles, are facts still fresh in the memories of those who, like the connoisseurs in De Quincey's famous essay, regard murder as a fine art. Strangely enough, the murderer having done his work, was afraid to leave the country. He declared that he had not intended to take the director's life, but only to stun and rob him and that, finding the blow had killed, he dared not fly for fear of drawing down suspicion upon his own head. As a mere robber he would have been safe in the States, but as a murderer he would inevitably have been pursued and given up to justice. So he forfeited his passage, returned to the office as usual at the end of his leave, and locked up his ill-gotten thousands till a more convenient opportunity. In the meanwhile he had the satisfaction of finding that Mr. Dwerrihouse was universally believed to have absconded with the money, no one knew how or whither.

Whether he meant murder or not, however, Mr. Augustus Raikes paid the full penalty of his crime, and was hanged at the Old Bailey in the second week in January, 1857. Those who desire to make his further acquaintance may see him any day (admirably done in wax) in the Chamber of Horrors at Madame Tussaud's exhibition, in Baker Street. He is there to be found in the midst of a select society of ladies and gentlemen of atrocious memory, dressed in the close-cut tweed suit which he wore on the evening of the murder, and holding in his hand the identical life-preserver, with which he committed it.

[From *Mixed Sweets from Routledge's Annual* (London: Geo. Routledge and Sons, 1867).]

Ars Necronomica 2024: A Portal into Bleakness and Wonder

Providence, RI: Providence Arcade, 1-30 August 2024

> I am sick of the old conventions,
>   And critics who will not praise,
> So sing ho for the open spaces,
>   And aesthetes with kindly ways.

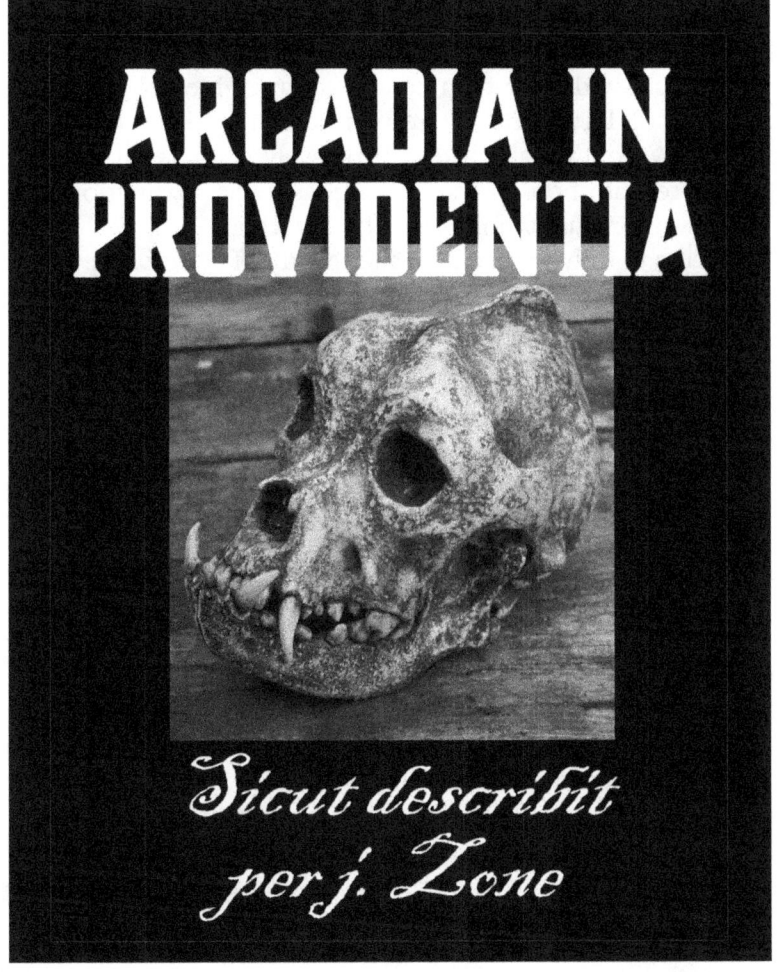

In between the partially cobbled streets of Westminster and Weybosset in downtown Providence stands a noble example of Greek Revival architecture birthed in 1828. The two flanks of this edifice facing those thoroughfares boasts six Cyclopean Ionic columns measuring 45 feet high. These were quarried, then brought from eight miles away in Johnston, Rhode Island, over dirt roads by teams of oxen. The Providence, or Westminster, Arcade has been the home of Lovecraft Arts & Sciences since 2015, and this year it hosted the 2024 edition of Ars Necronomica.

The last time this reviewer was there, the inside of the Arcade was fairly empty besides the LA&S store and one other business. It was extremely heartening to see that was no longer the case, with new commercial ventures Hey Neighboring the Hub of RI Weird. There was no Artist Guest of Honor this year (Gou Tanabe had preemptively been profiled in the Con's program book). And although a "fuller" exhibition than 2022 was promised initially, The Lovecraft Arts & Science Council had only invited a smaller group of twenty-five artists with just forty pieces among them. In previous iterations of ARS, it had been the curators' practice to reveal the originals of fine work done to promote the event. If done this year, that would have been originals by RI muralist Michael Ezzell and NJ's finest Kurt Komoda, but those were not to be seen. And yet the show seemed stronger. The content of about half of the pieces was Lovecraftian, but the high quality of the work was more responsible for elevating the whole presentation to a level better than the previous.

Regulars contributing consisted of Nick Gucker who summoned "The Dweller Beyond the Threshold," oozing forth midst an ichor of bejeweled acrylic; Liv Rainey-Smith (Without Whom It Wouldn't Be ARS . . .) with her latest woodcut depicting "Humanity Uplifted"—by Mi-Go (as you do); Jason McKittrick resonating with "The Seal of Cthulhu"; Josh Yelle (attendees were chuffed to see Thee Pencilmancer in full force after his early departure due to Covid in 2022) accompanied by "Biddy" in all her mixed media finery; and Mike Knives curating Cultist Couture with his window dressing of "Vvvfurrkgk, The Esteemed Vice-Regent Orator of The Nameless One."

Former Artist Guest of Honor Santiago Caruso returned with three works and provided a highpoint for me and others with his take on Clark Ashton Smith's "Tale of Satampra Zeiros." Other submissions included that by Matthew Jaffe ("The Death of Pan," a gorgeous sepia composition illustrating the Lord Dunsany tale); the Expressionist stylings of Victoria Dalpe; and Gris-gris gathered by one of this year's GoHs, Billy Martin.

In addition, were notable pieces by Ryan Lesser ("The Gate," more resin) and Paul Barton ("Priest of Leng," more ichor). The dark charcoal command of the aptly surnamed Brett Gray has been a mainstay of the horror scene for years and this year we were graced by his "Child of Cthulhu." Jennifer Hrabota Lesser unleashed "The Acolyte," a feral flipped version of the cultist that organizers were blessed to have represent the 2017 NecronomiCon campaign. Bob Eggleton, a true Son of Providence—who also is THE Kaiju Master—took sail in a sea of sumptuous oils 'round a shard of R'lyeh in "Titanus Cthulhu," an example proving that True Art by him and others such as Caruso leaves even the concept of AI-generated work unworthy for drydock. The artistry of Kelly Kotulak of Hibernacula Studios returned to the convention after she last submitted artwork to the 2015 Program Guide, with an "Alchemical Orchid" bringing a resplendent eldritch flash in its filigree. As a crowning touch, Gage Prentiss of the Rumtucket Trading Company had acquired the "Newman Cemetery Skull" in an East Providence estate sale and graciously lent it to serve as a literal cornerstone to this year's show. This relic alone attests to the continued aesthetic influence of Richard Upton Pickman's oeuvre over the entire Commonwealth, down through the Rhode Island plantations . . .

While this edition of Ars Necronomica was not in either of the polished halls of the Providence Art Club or the Woods-Gerry, the "pop-up" gallery adjacent to Lovecraft Arts & Sciences no doubt reinforced commercial as well as convivial interests more easily in its café-like atmosphere. One could list, for example, a personal recommendation by *Washington Post* luminary and bookman Michael Dirda for a novel by Walter de la Mare. Or the banter with a former co-curator and artist over déshabillé in convention deportment—the debate sweetened by baklava.

This year's Experience in the Divine City was comprised of many discussions, many conversations. Talk may have been cheap, but oh so priceless. The Children of Cthulhu dream of 2026.

"Child of Cthulhu" by Brett Gray.

Here every bard is a genius,
    And artists are Raphaels,
    And above the roofs of Patchin Place
        The Muse of Talent dwells.
—*H. P. Lovecraft*, "Arcadia" (Summer of 1935)

The Canadian Brick Wall

Géza A. G. Reilly

MICHAEL KELLY, ed. *Northern Nights*. N.p.: Undertow Publications, 2024. 296 pp. $19.99 tpb. ISBN: 9781988964478.

I wanted to enjoy *Northern Nights*. An anthology of all-Canadian horror fiction following in the lineage of previous anthologies by other editors such as *Northern Suns*, *Northern Stars*, and *Northern Frights*? Yes, please. I love American horror fiction, and I love horror fiction from countries I've never been to before (shoutout to Australia, which can produce some *very* messed-up horror), but there's just something about the idea of horror coming straight from the land of my birth. What a shame, then, that I'm honestly not certain that I can recommend *Northern Nights*.

My waffling isn't due to a lack of quality on offer. Indeed, many if not most of the stories in the anthology are excellent and memorable. A wide array of authors from all over the truly massive nation of Canada were chosen, and they've done an admirable job of presenting unique (and sometimes uniquely *Canadian*) terrors. And, as my previous parenthetical should suggest, there *is* a lot of Canada itself in this slim volume—sometimes, I fear, a bit too much for a non-Canadian reader. Still, I came away from *Northern Nights* with a sense that the project had run aground somewhere.

Let's first talk about the stories-as-stories that resonated with me. They start strong with Nayani Jensen's "Rescue Station," which is a particularly nasty *conte cruel*. Simon Strantzas's "The Needle Song" veers from the spare, tense prose of Jensen and runs wildly into a tale of horror mixed with coming-of-age narrative that reminded me of a 1980s episode of *The Outer Limits*. EC Dorgan's "Prairie Teeth" brings what I can only describe as a Canadian feminist take on a classic American country music tale to the table. "Fancy Dad" by David Nickles brought a sense of high weirdness to the volume that drove me to hunt online for actual local legends upon which it could have been based. Rory Say's "The Key to Black Creek" gives a wonderful take on weird fiction and underworld histories within the more easily ignored Canadian small towns. David Neil Lee's "The Church and the Westbound Train" is a lovely little vampire story wrapped up in the unique qualities of Canadian history. And Rich Larson's "DO NOT OPEN" and A. C. Wise's "The Slow Music of Drums" are truly bizarre bits of strangeness that left me desperately wanting more.

So the stories are, overall, good. There's a wide range of different types of horror here, and all the authors—even the ones whose work didn't resonate with me—are skilled at their craft. Why, then, was I left without much of an impression of *Northern Nights* other than a shrug of the shoulders and a muttered "that was okay"? Perhaps it was because of the very thing that had attracted me to the anthology in the first place: its Canadian-ness. An admirable amount of Canadian territory and life is offered here. Stories are set from British Columbia to the Maritimes, and even if a bit too many of them are set in Northern Ontario (and few, if any, are set in the oft-overlooked Manitoba), I can't complain about only presenting a small piece of the wider Canadian puzzle. Equally, the broad spectrum of our fundamentally multicultural society fills these pages, with First Nations peoples being featured here, as are immigrants, majority populations of all races and creeds, and, to my pleasant surprise, marginalized groups from Canadian history. And yet, I think there is a broader issue here. What does it mean, exactly, to be Canadian? How are we as a set of peoples distinct from others—particularly our southern neighbors? That, it seems, is a tricky question to answer.

I read an essay by a scholar many years ago (was it Robert Kroetsch? George Bowering?) that argued that if the postmodern condition was to center a stained-glass window between the individual and the world, then the *Canadian* postmodern condition was to center a brick wall between the individual and the world. The question of what the Canadian identity actually *is* has been longstanding; some have even proposed that the search for a Canadian identity *is* the Canadian identity. Earle Birney famously wrote in his poetry that we as a people are only defined by what we are not: we are *not*

Americans, we are *not* British, we are *not* French, etc. *Northern Nights* seems to fall into that exact trap. The landscapes on offer are unquestioningly Canadian, but the people within those landscapes? The events they are going through? How are *they* uniquely Canadian? I couldn't put my finger on how they are, and though I can't quite blame the authors for being unable to solve this particular problem of Canadian identity, it still gnawed at me as I read.

Even setting the question of Canadian identity aside, there is a chance that the stories in *Northern Nights* might be *too* Canadian for non-Canadian readers. Bear with me here: Canada has a long and storied history—one that is often unknown to those from other countries. How, then, would non-Canadians read and understand, say, K. L. Shroeder's "Lightbringers" if they don't know about the recent nationwide scandal of murdered and vanished First Nations women that rocked Canada as a whole? Would someone who knows nothing about the Riel Rebellion be able to take the subtleties of David Neil Lee's "The Church and the Westbound Train"? How opaque is Marc A. Godin's "Mi-Carême" to someone who is unaware of plight of the Acadian people and Father Le Loutre's War against the British (a subject I'd hazard not even many Canadians know about)?

Ultimately, the question becomes whether *Northern Nights* is meant to showcase Canadian horror fiction or if it is intended to showcase Canadian horror fiction *to other Canadians*. If the former, I don't think it quite succeeds for the reasons outlined here. If the latter, however, I don't think it quite succeeds there either—because what, ultimately, is the point? The stories in *Northern Nights* are fine, and if a reader is simply curious about what the Great White North has to offer in terms of home-grown horror, then by all means pick up the anthology. For the most part, you won't be disappointed. But I admit that I had hoped to be moved by this anthology—to be swept up in the currents and streams of the land of my birth, and that simply did not happen. As is the case with perhaps all Canadian culture, *Northern Nights* ultimately left me feeling as though I could see the outline of what Canada is, but not the living heart of it. Would that I could have seen more.

A Truly Haunting Haunting

Darrell Schweitzer

A Ghost Story. 2017. Written and directed by David Lowry. Starring Casey Affleck, Rooney Mara, and Will Oldham. 92 minutes.

I bring this film to your attention because I've never heard of it before, and would not have heard of it if my wife hadn't discovered it on a streaming channel. (I think it was Netflix.) It got no attention within the weird fiction community, for all that it may have won a bunch of critical awards. Audiences don't seem to have paid much attention either.

But it's a gem. Not to be confused with *Ghost Story,* which is based on the Peter Straub book. This is a very quiet, understated film, with very little dialogue, with lots of still shots, about a woman who likes to hide notes in places she has lived, to leave a bit of herself behind. Then her husband is killed in an auto accident. In the morgue, he is covered with a sheet. He wakes up as a ghost, beneath that sheet. This is his costume for the rest of the film, just the sheet, with two dark eyeholes and nothing showing in them. He follows his wife home, invisible to her, unable to communicate. He lingers. She grieves, then gets on with her life, and eventually begins seeing another man. Jealous, the ghost rattles things in the house. The widow writes a note, slips it into the wall, and paints over it. The ghost scratches at the wall, but cannot get the note out. His ex-wife moves away. A Spanish mother and her children move in. Jealous again, that they have made his house theirs, he starts throwing dishes. A third occupant holds a party, and as someone gives a long, pretentious speech about the futility of existence, the lights blink.

Now, presumably because the house is haunted, it is abandoned. The ghost makes contact with another ghost (in a floral sheet) in the house next door, who is waiting for someone but can't remember who or why. When both houses are demolished by a bulldozer, the floral ghost vanishes. Its sheet drops to the ground. But our ghost hangs on until other things are built on the spot and in the future skyscrapers rise into a dark sky like something out of *Bladerunner*. Despairing, our ghost leaps off a ledge and falls back in time, to a grassy meadow in the nineteenth century where a pioneer family are building the first cabin on the site. And so on. The ghost, still invisible and voiceless, lingers up into his own time, until a time-loop has occurred and he can see himself alive, then himself as a ghost and the grieving widow. He scratches the wall for the note . . .

This film is like a melancholy poem. You will watch it in still silence, never for an instant frightened, because this is not a scary film, but *haunted* because it is a hauntingly memorable one. That may be why audiences didn't really take to it (although according to Wikipedia it made a profit, $2 million on a $100,000 budget). Not a horror film. No jump effects. No monster faces. No blood and gore. But dark and lovely, about longing and loss.

Cultists Invade Providence: Reflections on NecronomiCon 2024

David T. Zeppieri

It was a sweltering August evening when we all filed into the ancient church. The house of worship felt oddly larger on the inside than it appeared from without. Wooden pews creaked, men sniffled and sweated, a pungent odor filling the air. Much as in H. P. Lovecraft's "The Festival," we were all eager for the ceremony to begin.

The festivities started with a bang, both literally and figuratively, as a massive thunderstorm struck the downtown area of Providence just as the organist began playing a spirited rendition of Bach's "Toccata and Fugue." You may have heard the piece before, but I assure you it is entirely different to experience it bellowing out from the pipes of a centuries-old organ, the bass notes reverberating through the entire building. And it is another thing entirely to have the piece punctuated by flashes of lightning and bolts of thunder!

As a wailing fire engine rushed past the Baptist Meeting House, there was a very real feeling that the Great Tentacled One truly had arisen from his watery grave of R'lyeh! And that eldritch feeling continued throughout the weekend, as fellow devotees of the Old Gentleman invaded downtown Providence, turning the capital city into as much of a haunted abode as the fictional Arkham, Massachusetts.

This was my first time attending a NecronomiCon convention, and I must say that it did not disappoint. Indeed, the convivial atmosphere, along with being surrounded by fellow fans of the Old Gentleman, was worth the price of admission alone! But far beyond that, the panels, films, and other programming offerings were such that a fellow could wish for some sort of reality-warping rune to allow him to experience everything that the gathering had to offer. As I am currently without a shining trapezohedron, I had to make due with merely the time allowed for us mortals.

The first stop at any convention is—of course—the dealers' room, and Necronomicon's did not disappoint. Artistry, antiquity, modernity, and all things cosmic horror were well-represented here. The Call of Cthulhu table-top game alone had an appropriately massive presence; yet so did all manner of publications from publishers both large and small. I gladly filled my satchel with semi-professional zines, vintage pulp paperbacks, and classic horror literature—enough reading material to last a good long while.

The panels were filled with an appropriately esoteric collection of topics, ranging from small-press magazines of yesteryear and hypothetical legal ramifications of the mythos (can Nyarlathotep be sued for patent infringement? does an attack by Cthulhu count as an "act of god"?) to the history of the Flat Earth belief, and even an in-depth look at deep-sea parasites (complete with gruesome photographs). It is heartening to discover that so many cosmic horror fans have an interest in such academic topics, judging from the rooms filled to capacity at several of these panels. I'm sure that Lovecraft himself would appreciate the deep dives into forgotten lore that so many of these scholars have taken!

I do regret missing out on many of the film screenings—particularly the potpourri of short films on offer—but I was fortunate enough to take in a showing of the "Colour out of Space"–inspired *Die, Monster, Die!* Although I'd seen the movie before, watching it with a live audience was a great experience. Titters of laughter washed over the auditorium in response to the hammy acting and questionable special effects. A fun time for sure!

A major highlight of the whole weekend was the Eldritch Ball. Held in the top-floor ballroom of the historic Graduate Hotel in the heart of downtown Providence, it felt every bit like attending a lavish gala at the haunted Overlook Hotel of *Shining* fame. Indeed, stepping out from the (frighteningly rickety) old elevator, the eerie sounds of Al Bowlly's "Midnight, the Stars, and You" echoed through the palatial ballroom—the perfect greeting to a night of spooky revelry! I was pleasantly surprised to see that the vast majority of attendees at the ball were dressed to the nines for the occasion—a sea of suits, tuxedos, gowns, and even a few monstrous costumes were all on display. In my gray suit and detective fedora I felt right at home!

Far more than just a boozy soirée, this was a true ball with dancing and musical accompaniment. Initially the tunes were much akin to those I am familiar with from my old Goth nightclub days; but this soon transitioned to live music performed by a spirited duo on drums and synthesizer. This made for excellent music to dance with a spooky filly or two, and really made the place come alive with true eldritch energy.

The ball also hosted live entertainment, in the form of interpretative dances inspired by Lovecraft's "The Colour out of Space"—which served as the general theme of the evening. While the first two performances were quite tasteful, the third and final one was a true burlesque dance in the classy, old-time tradition. I do wonder what ol' Howard would have thought about a burlesque show inspired by one of his most famous tales!

I would be remiss if I neglected to mention the Dark Adventure Radio Theatre and their wonderful production of *The Temple of Jupiter Ammon,* an original tale brimming with swashbuckling action in the vein of the pulps of yore. It is incredible that there is still a group putting on audio dramas in the style of old-time radio shows; and it was quite enjoyable to see the production live. There were even many moments of audience participation, with the projector screen calling upon the attendees to provide sound effects for howling desert winds, rushing underwater rivers, and grunting troglodytes!

No trip to Providence is complete without attending Waterfire. Although the event is held only a few times per year, NecronomiCon attendees were fortunate that the director of the event is a big fan of Lovecraft. While it was never stated outright, I have a sneaking suspicion that the mid-August Waterfire was put on purely for NecronomiCon attendees. Shoring up my hypothesis was a surprise visit from the Deep Ones in the middle of the festivities—costumed revelers waving their tentacles at the crowds from the bow of boats restocking the burning braziers up and down the canals. I have no doubt that the majority of Waterfire attendees had no idea who these strange fellows were supposed to be; but for Cthulhu Mythos fans it was a fun treat to see the denizens of Innsmouth making an appearance in the capital city!

Perhaps I have been overly complimentary in my event commentary; but it is difficult not to gush when a convention offers a unique opportunity to commune with such a small but dedicated fandom. If you're considering attending the next NecronomiCon but are on the fence about going, I wholeheartedly recommend you take the plunge and sign up. While it will be another two years until the next one, it is well worth waiting for when the stars are right once again.

The Lingering Shadow of World War II

S. T. Joshi

RAMSEY CAMPBELL. *The Incubations*. London: Flame Tree Press, 2024. 230 pp. £20 hc (UK), $26.95 (US). ISBN: 9781787589292.

We in the United States have led a blissfully sheltered existence when it comes to attacks by external enemies. Bypassing the dreadful single-day incident of 9/11 (and setting aside the incalculable devastation of our Civil War of 1861–65), we have to go all the way back to the war with Great Britain of 1812–14 to come upon a time when our country was actually invaded by a foreign foe.

England and Europe have not been so lucky. The two world wars of the twentieth century resulted in untold misery for nearly everyone who was alive during that time, and the relics of the destruction that unrelenting bombing caused can still be seen across the continent. The German blitz of 1940–41 left scars in England that have not yet healed, while the Allies' appallingly cruel and needless bombing of Dresden and other German cities even as the Nazis were on their last legs cannot be called anything but a war crime.

Ramsey Campbell was born a year after the conclusion of World War II, but I do not recall any major work in which he addresses the devastation—physical and psychological—of that conflict. That has all changed with his new novel, *The Incubations*.

At the outset we hardly seem to be dealing with war wounds. Leo Parker, a driving instructor, experiences inexplicable slips of the tongue ("Bulfinch Terror" for "Bulfin Terrace") that would be funny—and will no doubt drive translators to distraction—were it not that these verbal tics are interpreted by his client, Lucy Fenton, as making fun of her own dyslexia. She is so flustered that she cannot take a scheduled driving test. Leo himself now finds some difficulty in operating a vehicle—a serious threat to his livelihood. His father, Brian, who founded the business (Pass With Parker), has to take over Leo's pupils.

Meanwhile, Leo sees a psychologist, Anita Chattopadhyay, to see if he can get to the bottom of his anomalous ailment. He recounts an incident from his childhood where he and a friend, Billy Wallace, broke into a deserted munitions factory that had been bombed during the war. As he is horsing around in the property, Billy ends up dying in a hideous accident ("The end of the metal beam had rammed deep into his head, leaving no room for a face"). Leo naturally feels guilty, although he cannot possibly have been responsible for his friend's demise.

The town near Liverpool in which Leo lives, Settlesham (it is fictitious), is a "twin" city with a German town, Alphafen (also fictitious), which had been senselessly bombed by the Allies. The idea was to seek reconciliation after the war by emphasizing the common humanity of the people in both countries, and Leo participated in writing to a citizen of Alphafen, Hanna Weber; indeed, he was the only one in Settlesham who continued to write to his penpal after others had given up the task. Now Leo takes his first trip to the German city, where he meets Hanna and her parents, Emil and Gitte.

It is at this point that Campbell's patented ability to create unease through ambiguous dialogue comes to the fore. While outwardly friendly, there is a sinister undercurrent in what the Germans say in response to Leo's comments and queries about their town. Is it simply that their English is not quite up to grade? Leo is lavishly treated to a dinner in which the citizens of the entire city appear to be present; but he learns from an English tourist, Jerome Pugh (who turns out to be something of a neo-Nazi), that Hitler was in Alphafen—and, indeed, for some mysterious reason found it of especial interest. An embittered German man, Dietrich Gebhardt, confronts Leo: "Your bombs were meant to cast down Hitler, but they raised his spirits." Indeed, it appears that the bombing was "some sort of sacrifice."

Jerome Pugh later meets up with Leo in England, making cryptic remarks about the effect of the English bombing of

Alphafen: "The creatures must have taken all those deaths for nourishment." What creatures are these? It appears that "Alp" does not only refer to a mountain; Leo finds that "the alp [is] a nightmare creature . . . [that] might be related to the elf," and that it induces nightmares. What are we to make of the butterfly that flew into Leo's face when he was in Alphafen (a name that could well mean "refuge of the alp"), and that appears to have somehow been caught in his luggage as he returns to England? Why is it that, after he gives a lecture—illustrated by the photographs he took with his mobile phone—the photographs have all disappeared?

Most dreadful of all, there is every reason to believe that Leo had "infected someone with dread." Could the townspeople of Alphafen have infected Leo so that he "would be used to take their revenge on Settlesham"? From this point onward, things become increasingly harried and alarming for Leo. He feels he must destroy his phone, which may be the conduit for the creatures that are incubating within him; but this only leads to trouble with the police. His parents are afflicted with baffling ailments. But when he tells his girlfriend, Ellen, of his suspicions, she understandably scoffs and presents an elaborate psychological explanation of the whole situation. But then Jerome Pugh makes a dramatic and chilling warning about the alps:

> "They're the essence of the dark. They come up from the caves under the mountains and bring their darkness with them. Not a dark you can see, one you can feel. It feels as if you're trapped where there's never any light with things that need the dark to live in, and they delight in making you more afraid. It's what they feed on."

The Incubations may be one of Ramsey Campbell's quieter horror novels, but its relentless accumulation of unnerving details makes it a fearsomely compelling read from beginning to end. Campbell performs an exquisite dance between psychological terror and supernatural dread, and the plight of his well-meaning protagonist is keenly etched in a way that will cause every reader to feel for him and hope he can triumph over his baffling affliction—but with little confidence that he will do so. Lurking behind it all is the lingering shadow of Hitler's war, a cataclysm that has indelibly scarred the people and the nations that were dragged into it.

Ramsey Campbell, who is celebrating the sixtieth anniversary of the publication of his first book, shows with *The Incubations* that he remains the premier writer of weird fiction in our time, and perhaps of all time.

Portable Gothic: A Few Thoughts on Place

Karen Joan Kohoutek

Traditional Gothic tales have a relationship to place, both natural and man-made, that is alien to the experience of most modern people, especially Americans. From the time of the early English-language tales of fear and the supernatural, the norm has shifted from pastoral settings to urban ones, from rootedness to rootlessness.

The quintessentially haunted place is a moonlit night, with tree branches swaying in the wind, colored by fog and shadow, in a graveyard near an old church. The nighttime natural world and its elements strike the imagination as somehow purposeful and sinister, set in a place where human mortality is picturesquely invoked. When these elements entered the vocabulary of fright, they depicted a reality that people might see in their everyday lives, not something set in a past known only from frightening fictions. It makes sense that these symbols would survive, however, because they continue to evoke the right mood.

The "natural" trappings of the *Goblinstoria* come to be viewed as somehow unnatural. Besides the moon and the trees, we find clouds, wind, fog, and of course the thunderstorms of cliché. Even the corpse and the skeleton are part of nature. And what is more natural than the night? It comes around every day, all our lives. In part, the potential uncanniness lies in the sense that these elements are imbued or endowed with significance we cannot help putting on them. That is, it is not just a storm, it is a portent. It is not a regular fog, but one that obscures evil deeds. The tree branches in *Wuthering Heights*, for example, seem to have purpose in their movements. Normally mute, inanimate objects seem to take part in human events, motivated by human powers and emotions, or so it seems under the susceptibility of the spooked.

In the old-school Gothic, man-made elements are similarly

dramatic: castles, abbeys, ruined ancestral homelands. In discussions of the genre, scholars often begin with ideas from architecture and landscape, which later had an influence upon literature. The era reflected, for example, in Jane Austen's *Northanger Abbey* and the works of Ann Radcliffe was absolutely tied to specific places, usually with their own family histories and backgrounds of tragedy. But now, how many of us have an ancestral homeland? Even the phrase "haunted house" is more now associated with the funhouse Halloween entertainment and, with a few notable exceptions, the modern horror film is rarely set in an archetypal haunted castle.

Instead, we are in the era of the haunted mind. If, as some psychoanalytic theory suggests, the house generally does represent the human mind, its loss as a central symbol may have some significance. Without a metaphor of home, is the average person abandoned to a fragmented identity? Without a haunted space, are the ghosts, the things we repress and those we fear, roaming the world unfettered?

Of course, many people still live with strong ties to extended families and the places where they grew up. But many of us are more mobile now than the old-time tellers of ghost stories could ever have imagined. For those who move frequently and put down no real roots, their only site is the self. The burden of hauntedness is upon the individual. It is they who wander alone among old mental graveyards, looking for markers, but finding them faded, the weeds grown over, the stones worn away. That is largely the world of ideas we have inherited.

The yearning for place still exists, and the desire to be steeped in the kind of atmosphere that wraps around a specific place and a definable history. That is why places like Salem, New Orleans, and Whitby are Gothic meccas. For most, however, apart from a population of longtime locals, they are adopted homelands, spiritual ones, not based on one's real history with the sites.

On the level of the house, to be considered "haunted," even in a very casual way, the space requires a sense of continued history. People—the observers, the storytellers, the audience—need to stay in one place long enough for the idea to be passed along. The physical place has to remain unchanged for a length of time. And at the bottom of these conditions, people need to know their neighbors. A place can be creepy, but in a social vacuum it will never blossom into a story. There are still going to be communities, mostly smaller ones, with relatively stable populations, where the abandoned and unusual can grow into legends, even if not literally urban ones. But more and more, these conditions are becoming uncommon.

This is not to say there will not always be places to serve as foci for eeriness. There will always be houses that appear to be mysteriously abandoned or otherwise ill-starred. People's imaginations can easily light upon a darkened old building and interpret it as spooky. More often than not, now, that is clearly a kind of projection, based on an individual perception rather than any external knowledge. The abandoned house in my small hometown could be haunted in lore, but the one across the street in Minneapolis was haunted only in my imagination. The next people who moved into my apartment would have no way to know how long it had been empty, or what experience gave me the impression of something unusual.

In general, the traditional Gothic settings—old houses, ruins, cemeteries—become haunted by history as time and decay work their magic. We can still guess that something happened there, but too often, we no longer know what. Our hauntings are transient, and we carry our Gothic lens with us from place to place.

Updating Blackwood's "The Willows"

Darrell Schweitzer

T. KINGFISHER. *The Hollow Places*. New York: Saga Press, 2020. 341 pp. $17.99 tpb. ISBN: 9781534451124.

An advantage, even for book reviewers, of belonging to an informal book club is that you are led to read things you might otherwise have missed. I discovered T. Kingfisher (a.k.a. Ursula Vernon) through such a group, first with one of her humorous fantasies, *A Wizard's Guide to Defensive Baking* (2020), which is, in a word, delightful, all about a young girl who has to defend her native city when all the other wizards have been purged. The problem is, her specialty is baking. She can make dough rise in interesting ways, but how does that help against the hordes of the ungodly? It's a very funny, touching book.

This was something of a necessary catch-up for me. One of the things you realize as you get older is that there are more books than you will ever be able to read in a lifetime, and some of them have to be allowed to pass by. I am seventy-two and, goodness, I have never read Herodotus or S. Fowler Wright (whom Lovecraft recommends as one of the three writers known to him producing adult level science fiction) or a large bulk of the work of Mark Twain. There is even one Lord Dunsany book I have not read. Meanwhile, Ursula Vernon has since about 2009 produced a great quantity of books for children and adults, and won (count 'em) *five* Hugo Awards, two Nebulas, a Locus Award, and three Mythopoeic Awards, with many more nominations. This rather hints at a writer worth noticing. True, in the wake of the Puppies and anti-Puppies, the Hugos in particular have become politicized and have lost a good deal of their cachet; but still, there is an obvious trend here.

So, thankfully, the book discussion group got me to read *The Hollow Places*, and the reason I am writing about it four years after its publication is that it is *really good*. Vernon has not written a lot of horror fiction, but what she has sounds intriguing. *The Twisted Ones* (2019), which I have not read, is described as a "modern take" on Arthur Machen's "The White People." That is very interesting in itself. *The Hollow Places* is a similar "take" on Algernon Blackwood's "The Willows." If you are one of those people who reads introductions and afterwords (all the short stuff) before plunging into a novel proper, you might be a little put off by Vernon's statement that, even though H. P. Lovecraft wrote that "The Willows" was "one of the most terrifying stories every written" (which you and I know it is), before she read it she "assumed that this probably meant that some of the people in it weren't white, and I began preparing to roll my eyes a bit." This tells us that Vernon knows very little about Lovecraft and suggests that she is making a series of belated discoveries as she gropes her way through the canon of weird fiction. (I think she particularly needs to read Lovecraft's "Supernatural Horror in Literature" to get an idea of what's out there.)

But her novel is nowhere near as naïve as that statement. It is one of the most vivid and creepiest supernatural novels I have read in a long time, with characters you actually care about, rather than victims lined up to be sliced and diced (a problem I have with some of Clive Barker's work, for instance). We meet Kara, a.k.a. Carrot, a thirty-something recent divorcée still being bothered by her irritating ex, who has moved in with her uncle in Hog Chapel, North Carolina, where he manages the Glory to God Museum of Natural Wonders, Curiosity, and Taxidermy. The museum is itself a character, one of those labyrinthine accumulations of the strange and humorously incongruous that abound in fantasy fiction and we hope to find in real life. (If you're ever in Culver City, California, check out the Museum of Jurassic Technology. That's the real deal. There is a Cockroach Hall of Fame somewhere in the Midwest, if that's your thing. And of course the ultimate example of this particular art form is the House on the Rock in Wisconsin, as made famous in Neil Gaiman's *American Gods*. If the Glory to God Museum of Natural Wonders existed, it would be in such company.)

When Uncle Earl is laid up with knee surgery, Kara has to run the museum herself. She makes friends with Simon, the very out-of-the-closet gay operator of the coffee shop next door. That Simon is gay is quite relevant to the story: since Kara is in no position or mood for romance right now, she is able to bond with the charming Simon precisely because no romance is possible.

To this point, *The Hollow Places* is witty and fun, but it turns sinister very quickly when a hole is discovered in an upstairs wall, and through that hole is another world, first the inside of a concrete military bunker, then a world of water and low, flat islands and willow trees, the world of Blackwood's "The Willows"—not located on the Danube, but in another dimension, which connects to yet more dimensions. From one of these worlds, an army expedition entered and built the concrete bunkers, now in ruins, the expedition having apparently failed. In one, Kara and Simon find a corpse. In another, there is someone who is still alive but has met a hideous fate. (No more details than that. No spoilers.)

The place is indeed haunted by demonic, elemental forces, which make strange indentations in the sand, the way Blackwood described, and which can almost be glimpsed in the negative space between the trees (as Blackwood described in one of his most memorable bits, when great numbers of "spirits" are seen rising into the sky). Our heroes realize they are in terrible danger. The place will devour them. The problem is, all the bunkers and islands look alike, and Kara and Simon are soon lost. When they do make it back to their own world, about three-fifths of the way through the book, there is a temporary feeling of relief, but you know the story is not over and it is not, as something from the willow world invades the Museum and magically transforms it. The result is a painful, terrifying climax, and an explanation that may perhaps seem less than totally satisfactory. All this happened because of something that arbitrarily came in the mail, one more oddity donated to the museum. (More than that I will not say. Spoilers.) But what more than makes up for any weakness in plotting is the vividness of the writing. You can practically feel the damp and the slime and the crumbling rust (of the hatches on the bunkers). Vernon has a very good eye and ear for sinister detail, and a good sense of pacing, so that, even when the narrative temporarily relaxes, interest never flags. She even characterizes Kara's cat well. What more can you ask? You really *should* seek this book out and read it.

And I continue to wonder what would result if Vernon ever discovers Lovecraft in a serious way. She could do marvelous things with his material, I am sure.

"The Earth Alone Lasts:" The Myth of Meaning in the Speculative Fiction of Robert W. Chambers

Katherine Kerestman

ROBERT W. CHAMBERS. *Robert W. Chambers*. Ed. S. T. Joshi. (Masters of the Weird Tale.) Lakewood, CO: Centipede Press, 2023. 822 pp. $295.00 hc. ISBN: 9781613470602.

I had read Robert W. Chambers's *The King in Yellow* previously and found it to be a work of agreeably mind-boggling weird fiction; this well-known story group fuses fantastic and ancient literary forms and tropes with modern workaday life to create a delicious disconnect such as might be approximated by viewing the unicorn tapestries in Cluny and discovering a man talking on a cell phone in the woven wood. Now, in reading the collected stories in this Masters of the Weird Tale volume, I have happily discovered that throughout his weird tales Chambers's modern world is infused with monsters and magic and basted in irreverent wit and Swiftian satire. I envision Chambers twirling his moustache with éclat as his pen scratches the page. His diction, while elegant and upper-crust, sparkles with fairy words and jars complacency with ostentatious scientific jargon. This volume includes stories in which dreamscapes merge with academia and every female lead character possesses pouting red lips and is a scientist or detective to boot.

The introduction, by Joseph S. Pulver, Sr., is disappointing for the reason that it discusses only *The King in Yellow*. I would have enjoyed reading Pulver's thoughts on the other works in the hefty, oversized tome as well. Pulver's essay considers the central motifs of the four stories that make up *The King in Yellow;* but more interesting is his discussion of the bastardization of Chambers's work by August Derleth. Derleth credited Chambers with being a formative influence on the work of H. P. Lovecraft—even though Lovecraft had been writing for years before he first read Chambers. Derleth also haphazardly appropriated elements of both Chambers's and Lovecraft's work into his own "Cthulhu Mythos," warping them for his own purposes and gain. Pulver explains that this reprehensible "literary" trend has been continued since Derleth by some subsequent writers and members of the Cthulhu gaming community, be it intentionally or through ignorance.

Moving from Pulver's introduction to the stories of this collection, settings as banal as New York City and as alien as the unexplored regions of Canada and the Arctic are all dreamscapes in the author's hands. The nebulous nature of reality and unnerving hints of possible madness perfuse each tale: madness, visited upon the unwary who read the forbidden play *The King in Yellow*, is the major theme of the group of tales by the same name. Chambers's fantastic tales question the possibility of an objective reality: in "A Pleasant Evening," for instance, the narrator, a New York newspaper illustrator, delivers a note—given to him by a mysterious woman who tells him that he will know to whom he should give it—to an accused French traitor who shoots himself when he gets the note, written by his sweetheart who drowned while crossing the ocean to bring him proof of his innocence. Sent by his boss to sketch a picture of a corpse in the morgue, the illustrator discovers the corpse to be the mysterious woman with the note; she is smiling and clutching the same letter. Outside, he sees the mysterious woman dead on the ground with the dead soldier.

Such unsettling endings unhinge the reader's own understanding of the border that separates fiction from reality. In "The Maker of Moons" an artist's discovery of a mysterious brooch and crab-like creature lead to an adventure in the Canadian woods complete with Ysonde, a beautiful woman who carves inscrutable figures in golden balls; undercover special government agents on the trail of a manufactured-gold ring that threatens to overturn the world's economies; strange beings, such as the mouthless, eyeless crab-things with yellow hair and a "damp acrid odor. . . a nightmare—it's unclean!"; and Chinese sorcery and mythology that link civilized North

America to Yian, a city "where the river winds under the thousand bridges, where the gardens are sweet scented and the air is filled with the music of silver bells." After many twists and turns and dip into magical vistas, the fictional author's wife, Ysonde, rudely intrudes into our fantasy, to ask him how he can write such nonsense. Was all his testimony only a story? The text is so haunting that it is difficult for the reader to relinquish their willingly suspended belief so abruptly.

In *In Search of the Unknown,* the narrator, who is sent by the Bronx Zoo to an island on a mission to bring back some nearly extinct auks and to look into reports of a bipedal amphibious creature, prefaces his tale by saying that he has been promoted to Secretary of the Zoological Gardens. Upon this promotion, he has been advised by his colleagues to give up writing fiction to lend greater credence to his nonfiction work:

> To separate fact from fancy has always been difficult for me . . . Therefore it is to a serious and unimaginative public that I shall hereafter address myself; and I do it in the modest confidence that I shall neither be distrusted nor doubted, although unfortunately I still write in that irrational style which suggests covert frivolity, and for which I am undergoing a course of treatment in English literature at Columbia College. Now, having promised to avoid originality and confine myself to facts, I shall tell what I have to tell concerning the dengue, the mammoth, and *something else.*

Endings and beginnings generally blur imagination and fact. They are indistinct and distorted.

Chambers's women, like Ysonde, are mysterious and inscrutable creatures—animals difficult to comprehend; creatures that are loving but not always loving whom you would expect them to love; beautiful, soft, sonorous, scented, dreamlike entities; fascinating, intelligent scientists and musicians. In *In Search of the Unknown,* the stenographer is revealed to hold a doctorate in etymology and to be moonlighting between university jobs; the Countess Suzanne d'Alzette, who has five ux eggs in incubators, is struggling to get a hearing by the scientific community at the Paris Exhibition of 1900 so that she can present her proofs of the existence of the aforementioned ux. The waitress of "The Third Eye" is a school-teacher working her way toward a graduate degree and a Smithsonian appointment. The pretty girl in "The Ladies of the Lake" is a nurse with violet eyes who wears her uniform with a red cross on the sleeves on a ladies' expedition into uncharted territories; we learn that she is about to complete her studies for an M.D. and plans to make a eugenic marriage. Most of the stories in this volume, howsoever speculative in nature, are also screwball romantic comedies. To further confuse the indistinct line between genres—and between fiction and reality—when the narrator inevitably fails to get the girl, he moralizes in this manner:

> . . . the feminine assistant of Professor Jane Bottomly, who sauntered into my study and announced herself, had the features of Athene, the smile of Aphrodite, and the figure of Psyche. I believe I do not exaggerate these scientific details, although it has been said of me that any pretty girl distorts my vision and my intellectual balance to the detriment of my calmer reason and my differentiating ability.

Robert W. Chambers was a painter as well as a writer, and his stories are much richer for his facility with visual detail. Light and color receive remarkable treatment:

> Across the long meadow I could see the roofs of the city faintly looming above the trees. A mist of amethyst, ever deepening, hung low on the horizon, and through it, steeple and dome, roof and tower, and the chimneys where thin fillets of smoke curled idly, were transformed into pinnacles of beryl and flaming minarets, swimming in filmy haze. Slowly the enchantment deepened; all that was ugly and shabby and mean had fallen away from the distant city, and now it towered into the evening sky, splendid, gilded, magnificent, purified in the fiery furnace of the setting sun.
>
> The red disk was half hidden now; the tracery of trees, feathery willow and budding birch, darkened against the glow; the fiery rays shot far across the meadow, gilding the dead leaves, staining with soft crimson the dark moist tree trunks around me.

Texture and touch as well: "Like velvet rubbed on velvet the canoe brushed across the sand." And sound: "There are ghosts of sound which return to haunt long after sound is dead. It was these voiceless spectres of a voice long dead that stirred the transparent silence, intoning toneless tones." Sonorous, drowsy, Chambers's elongated, elegant sentences paint the mind with a dreamy mood.

In "The Yellow Sign," Chambers rhapsodizes on the power of words—the magical properties of lyrical etudes such the preceding excerpts:

> "Oh, the sin of writing such words [*The King in Yellow*],—words which are clear as crystal, limpid and musical as bubbling springs, words which sparkle and glow like the poisoned diamonds of the Medicis! Oh the wickedness, the hopeless damnation of a soul who could fascinate and paralyze human creatures with such words,—words understood by the ignorant and wise alike, words which are more precious than jewels, more soothing than music, more awful than death!"

Time is upended, not sequential in Chambers's worlds. In "Passeur," a man watching the clock, waiting for minutes to pass, fidgets to pass the time: "Time was disturbed in the room; the strands of shadows seemed entangled among the hands of the clock, dragging them back from their rotation. He wondered if the shadows would strangle Time, some still night when the wind and the flat river were silent."

My favorite story is "The White Shadow," a love story that takes place in a magic moment before a tragic accident; the romantic narrative, it gradually dawns upon the reader, is the lives they lived after death. Time is warped, twisted, fluid, and strange—but finite, for everything ends:

> When the winds stir the leaves among the poplars, and the long shadows fall athwart the fields; when the winds rise at night, and the branches scrape and crack above the moonlit snow; when in the long hot day the earth's bathed in fragrance, and all the little creatures of the fields are silent; when in the still evenings the flowers perfume the air, and the gravel walks shine white in the moonlight; when the breezes quicken

from the distant coast; when the sand shakes beneath the shock of the breakers, and every wave is plumed with white; when the calm eye of the beacon turns to mine, lingers, and turns away, and the surf is yeasty and thick; when I start at the sound of a voice from the cliffs, and my eyes are raised in vain; when the white gulls toss and drift in the storm-clouds and the water hurries out in the black ebb tide; when I rise and look from the window; when I dress, when I work with pen and colour; when I rest; when I walk; when I sleep—there is one face before my eyes, one name on my lips. For the white shadow is turning gray, and God alone knows the end.

Chambers draws the reader into enchanted realms and fantastic spaces, only to jar him out of his dream once he has settled comfortably into it. "A Pleasant Evening" (the narrative of the newspaper illustrator who delivers the note from the mysterious woman to the accused French traitor) is embedded within the story of his work assignment to sketch a corpse in the morgue, in the interests of sensational headlines built on a tragedy. The setting is New York City, which is characterized by a "*something* that gave the whole restless throng a common likeness—the expression of one who hastens toward a hopeless goal." The scientists who roam the world in search of unknown flora and fauna are repeatedly derided in *In Search of the Unknown,* wherein the best weapon to destroy a person's credibility is said to be ridicule; the comedy of this story group is centered largely upon scientific rivalries; and five august members of the scientific community and royal dignitaries sit on the ux eggs to hatch them. After relating the story told by a man he meets on a train about a great white cat (his reincarnated great-aunt) and how his girl would not marry him (because his great-aunt had kittens), followed by a discussion of Professor Farrago's marriage to a transparent woman (would their children be transparent? translucent?), the narrator explains:

> "The tremendous scientific importance of these experiences excited me beyond measure. The simplicity of the narrative, the elaborate attention to corroborative detail, all bore irresist-

ible testimony to the truth of these accounts of phenomena vitally important to the entire world of science . . . we lingered long in the dining-car, propounding questions, advancing theories, speculating upon possibilities of most intense interest."

The vanity of human wishes is most often illustrated by the fact that the protagonists of his funnier tales never get the girl, but in "The Carpet of Belshazzar," Dick, who shares a passion that has persisted through numerous lifetimes with Geraldine, must witness her abuse and death at the hands of her jealous husband. Although romance plays a large part in Chambers's various stories, it is always a doomed prospect. I am reminded of the nihilism of Queen's "Bohemian Rhapsody": "Nothing really matters." All the magic—including love—comes to an end in every story.

The Slayer of Souls concludes the volume. It is my least favorite, a novel of Secret Service agents fighting the Red Scare/Bolshevism/Anarchy, for which battle they recruit a young woman who lived in China during World War I until she was rescued by the Japanese invasion. In China, she learned Chinese magic when, following the massacre of her parents and other English-speaking people, she was sent to be a temple girl. The woman is deployed as a secret weapon, and Chinese mythology is turned against the Chinese and other revolutionaries who promote "violence toward those in authority." It is a didactic piece of wartime propaganda.

I have but scratched the surface of Chambers's fin de siècle literary brilliance. This volume is an indulgence in luxurious prose, a magic carpet flight of fancy, an opium dreamscape that, unfortunately, comes with a rude awakening.

When Everything Is Wrong and Nothing Is for Anyone

Géza A. G. Reilly

ROBERT GUFFEY. *The Expectant Mother Disinformation Handbook*. Gutter Mystic Books, 2024. 406 pp. $19.95 tpb. ISBN: 9781955745819.

The Expectant Mother Disinformation Handbook is an interesting read. It feels, in many ways, like a magic trick. I don't know if I'm going to revisit it anytime soon, but I can say that despite its length and lack of overall plot, it is an engaging, thought-provoking read.

Those of you who have taken my advice and snapped up a copy of Robert Guffey's collection *Cryptopolis* should be familiar with the rough outlines of *The Expectant Mother Disinformation Handbook*. A few excerpts from the present work were included in *Cryptopolis* as a standalone story. Those morsels, however, are nothing compared to the feast of the *Handbook* in full. Two-hundred and thirty-two entries populate these pages (ostensibly, and incorrectly, one for every day that an average pregnancy lasts). These entries range from the prosaic to the fantastic, from the weird to the horrific, from the poignant to the disgusting, and from the hilarious to the deplorable.

So what is *The Expectant Mother Disinformation Handbook*? Well, it is purportedly a guide put out by a society of some sort that is, perhaps stupidly, called *The Expectant Mother Disinformation Handbook*. What is this society and what are its goals? Who knows . . . sort of. There is an answer to those questions in the pages of the *Handbook*, but as with many things in Robert Guffey's writing, that answer might be nothing more than a gag.

Since there isn't any sort of plot and no real characters in this volume, I prefer to think of the text holistically. Let's start with the title. Notice how the use of "Mother" isn't in the possessive form? That caught my eye. What it suggests is that the *Handbook* isn't for the use of mothers, who a naïve person might assume would be the primary readership of a book on pregnancy. Since the *Handbook* isn't for them, then who is it for? Well, fathers, perhaps. They certainly do populate a good number of the entries in the book. Sometimes they have their questions answered, and sometimes they are addressed directly by the authors. But is the text as a whole *for* fathers?

I don't think so. And the reason I don't think so is another word in the title: "Disinformation." This *Handbook* is not intended to be a helpful guide as to what pregnancy is and what risks might be involved with a pregnancy. Instead, it is about what pregnancy is *not*. I found this a charming approach—Guffey has given us the *via negativa* of pregnancy handbooks. This is his attempt to pull a *Jacob's Room*, describing the subject at hand only by depicting the outlines that it has filled in the past. Pregnancy does *not* entail origami babies, or quantum superposition babies, or Hermetic cults obsessed with babies, or any of that stuff.

If pregnancy doesn't entail all of that—if it isn't about the High Weirdness being ladled up as thick servings of disinformation—then what does it actually entail? Well, let us return to the authors of the *Handbook* and who they wrote it for. If what those authors are presenting is wrong, and if they are presenting it to pretty much anyone but mothers themselves, then I think it follows that the *Handbook* is describing actual pregnancies carried by actual mothers in a negative space trick. It is saying, quite simply, that what happens during those *actual* pregnancies is nobody's business but the mothers. We, as an audience, are shut out from those realities, locked into the fantasies scrawled across each page, each entry, each wild-eyed question and equally wild answer, blinded by disinformation to such an extent that we can only see the reality of what is being discussed as an after-image.

We are nowhere involved in the topic at hand itself. Perhaps Guffey is saying that that is how it should be. Pregnancy, the alchemical miracle of the spontaneous generation of an actual, no kidding, for really real thinking and feeling human being is a wonderful thing that can be understood, be empathized with, be witnessed with joy ... but it isn't the domain of meddlers. It isn't supposed to be the space in the human experience where veritable Hall Monitors like the authors of the *Handbook* dip their beaks in and insist that pregnancy, fetuses, and mothers should be and behave in only the ways that *they* find acceptable. There is one road to righteousness, those authors suggest, and Guffey pulls a sorcerous spell by allowing us to understand just how delusional those with such presumptions are by the end of his text.

I really can't sugarcoat this one: By the time I was done with *The Expectant Mother Disinformation Handbook*, I absolutely loathed the fictional authors of these entries. I suspect that many people will feel the same way I did, for these authors are bigoted, prejudiced, intellectually dishonest, and generally the sort of people who can bring any party, no matter how wild, crashing to an uncomfortable halt. Sure, the thin narrative that runs through the *Handbook* brings them to a delightfully funny end toward the conclusion of the text, but that felt more like a release valve than any sort of pure narrative direction. If it weren't for that ending, I would have come out of the *Handbook* in a foul mood.

Instead, I was able to come out of it thinking, "Damn, that was hilariously strange. Thank God those bastards aren't real!" Even if they were real, they would still be wrong about everything and still be meddling in affairs that don't concern them. At this historical moment, when it comes to pregnancy and autonomy, we've got plenty of meddlers in our own prosaic existence. We've got plenty of people who think that they know best—better even than a given pregnant woman. We don't need more of them, but we could damn well use more examples of them turned into buffoons just like we get to see in the *Handbook*.

So I'm not sure I'll be revisiting *The Expectant Mother Disinformation Handbook* anytime soon. It is long, often directionless, and showcases some of the worst attitudes humanity can bring to one of the most innocent and beautiful things humanity is capable of doing. For all that, however, I'm glad it exists, and I'm glad that I had a chance to read it at least once. I recommend that others spend some time with it, too, for it is often weird, often funny, frightfully well written, and it gives us that unique satisfaction that only fiction can provide by putting the bastards into a magic circle of their own disinformation and locking them away. Isn't it sweet to think that they'd stay there.

About the Contributors

Michael Abolafia is a co-editor of *Dead Reckonings*.

Leigh Blackmore's horror fiction has appeared in more than sixty magazines from *Avatar* to *Strange Detective Stories*. He has reviewed for journals including *Lovecraft Annual, Shoggoth, Skinned Alive,* and *Dead Reckonings*. His critical essays appear in volumes including Benjamin Szumskyj's *The Man Who Collected Psychos: Critical Essays on Robert Bloch,* Gary William Crawford's *Ramsey Campbell: Critical Essays on the Modern Master of Horror*, Danel Olson's *21st Century Gothic,* and elsewhere. New weird verse has appeared in *Penumbra* and other journals.

Ramsey Campbell is an English horror fiction writer, editor, and critic who has been writing for well over fifty years. He is frequently cited as one of the leading writers in the field. His website is www.ramseycampbell.com.

Edward Guimont is Chair of the History and Social Science Department of Bristol Community College in Fall River, Massachusetts. He is also head of the academic speaker track at NecronomiCon Providence.

Amelia B. Edwards (1831–1892) was an English writer and Egyptologist best known for the ghost story *The Phantom Coach* (1864) and the travelogue of *Egypt a Thousand Miles Up the Nile* (1877).

Alex Houstoun is a co-editor of *Dead Reckonings*. He has published *Copyright Questions and the Stories of H. P. Lovecraft,* available by contacting him at deadreckoningsjournal@gmail.com.

S. T. Joshi is the author of *The Weird Tale* (1990), *I Am Providence: The Life and Times of H. P. Lovecraft* (2010), *Unutterable Horror: A History of Supernatural Fiction* (2012), and other critical and biographical studies. He has edited the work of H. P. Lovecraft, Lord Dunsany, Arthur Machen, Algernon Blackwood, Ambrose Bierce, and other weird writers.

Katherine Kerestman is the author of *Lethal* (PsychoToxin Press, 2023) and *Creepy Cat's Macabre Travels: Prowling around Haunted Towers, Crumbling Castles, and Ghoulish Graveyards* (WordCrafts Press, 2020), as well as the co-editor (with S. T. Joshi) of *The Weird Cat* and *Shunned Houses* (WordCrafts Press, 2023 and 2024). Her Lovecraftian and Gothic works have been featured in *Black Wings VII*, *Penumbra*, *Journ-E*, *Spectral Realms*, *Illumen*, *Retro-Fan*, *The Little Book of Cursed Dolls* (Media Macabre, 2023), as well as other discerning publications.

Karen Joan Kohoutek, an independent scholar and poet, has published about weird fiction in various journals and literary websites. Recent and upcoming publications have been on subjects including the Gamera films, the Robert E. Howard/H. P. Lovecraft correspondence, folk magic in the novels of Ishmael Reed, and the proto-Gothic writer Charles Brockden Brown. She lives in Fargo, North Dakota.

Géza A. G. Reilly is a writer and critic with an interest in twentieth-century American genre literature. A Canadian expatriate, he now lives in the wilds of Florida with his wife, Andrea, and their cat, Mim.

Darrell Schweitzer has been publishing weird or fantastic poetry for decades. Not counting comic verse, two previous collections of (mostly weird) verse are *Groping Toward the Light* (2000) and *Ghosts of Past and Future* (2008). *Dancing Before Azathoth*, a volume of previously and selected poems, is forthcoming from Hippocampus Press. His most recent story collection is *The Children of Chorazin* (Hippocampus Press, 2023) and his most recent anthology is *Shadows out of Time* (PS Publishing, 2023). *Dancing Before Azathoth: Macabre and Fantastic Poetry* is forthcoming from Hippocampus Press.

Joe Shea (The joey Zone) is an artist and illustrator. Samples of his work can be found at www.joeyzoneillustration.com.

David T. Zeppieri is a Connecticut yankee with a life-long interest in the mysterious and the unknown. He can regularly be found exploring historic New England cemeteries.

www.ingramcontent.com/pod-product-compliance
Lightning Source LLC
Chambersburg PA
CBHW071819020426
42331CB00007B/1551